UCHICAGO**CCSR**

THE UNIVERSITY
OF CHICAGO
CONSORTIUM ON CHICAGO
SCHOOL RESEARCH

I0083336

RESEARCH REPORT MAY 2013

Teens, Digital Media, and the Chicago Public Library

Penny Bender Sebring, Eric R. Brown, Kate M. Julian, Stacy B. Ehrlich, Susan E. Sporte, Erin Bradley, and Lisa Meyer

TABLE OF CONTENTS

Acknowledgements

As this was the first study the University of Chicago Consortium on Chicago School Research (UChicago CCSR) has undertaken of an out-of-school program, we want to give special thanks to the staff of YOUmedia Chicago at the Harold Washington Library Center. They welcomed us into their midst for three years, introduced us to digital media and other arts activities, and facilitated in every possible way the gathering of information. We also sincerely thank the hundreds of Chicago teens who allowed us to observe them as they participated in YOUmedia, filled out our questionnaires, and talked to us about their interests, activities, and creative endeavors. We benefited from the guidance provided by Amy Eshleman and Nichole Pinkard in framing our research questions. "Brother" Mike Hawkins and Taylor Bayless went far beyond the call of duty to help us arrange numerous events, ranging from meetings with the staff to census administrations. We are indebted to Kiley Larson for helping to develop relevant and clear survey questions. Kimberly Austin added greatly to our understanding of the field of digital media and learning. Mimi Ito inspired us to look deeply into youths' interests and how they pursue them, and she graciously reviewed a draft of this report, offering judicious advice on language use. We very much appreciate the time and input the UChicago CCSR Steering Committee provided. Two members of the committee, Mathew Stagner and Arie van der Ploeg, carefully reviewed the penultimate draft and pointed to questions not well answered and findings that should be elevated to better inform practitioners. Our UChicago CCSR colleagues, Elaine Allensworth, David Stevens, Bronwyn McDaniel, and Emily Krone, gave us invaluable advice that contributed to greater clarity of concepts and a more cogent narrative. We also acknowledge our summer intern, Ana Otcharova, who analyzed and summarized the travel patterns of teens to YOUmedia, thus illuminating its broad reach throughout the city.

Finally, we would like to thank Connie Yowell and An-Me Chung at the John D. and Catherine T. MacArthur Foundation for their continuous and generous support of UChicago CCSR, and in particular for pushing us to think in new directions about the relevance and necessity of research on digital media and learning.

This report was produced by UChicago CCSR's publications and communications staff: Emily Krone, Director for Outreach and Communication; Bronwyn McDaniel, Communications and Research Manager; and Jessica Puller, Communications Specialist.

Graphic Design: Jeff Hall Design
Photography: Cynthia Howe
Editing: Ann Lindner

05.2013/1,000/jh.design@rcn.com

to opportunities beyond YOUmedia. Their roles often extend beyond teaching or sharing their expertise. It is not surprising that more than two-thirds of a 200-person representative survey sample reported that they had a personal relationship with at least one mentor.

However, the design of the program, which privileges teen choice, poses challenges. In order to engage teens, adults deliberately seek out their interests and design workshops, projects, and theme-based sessions to appeal to their varied inclinations. Staff must cajole and persuade in order to attract teens to the workshops and projects where they can build their skills and deepen their expertise. Staff members have found it particularly difficult to encourage novice youth to develop the skills they need to take advantage of the high-profile events that are available to teens with more advanced skill levels.

Successful Replication of YOUmedia in Other Locations Will Depend on Both Local and Universal Conditions

YOUmedia's major programmatic partners are the Digital Youth Network, with its expertise working in schools and its strength in designing and providing learning activities, and the Chicago Public Library, with its history of offering open and free access to all of Chicago's youth. Joining such diverse partners into a working whole does not occur without hard work on the part of everyone involved. Others planning a similar initiative should be mindful of the need for frequent and regular communication and for the development of a shared set of practices. In addition, YOUmedia was fortunate to have a central location and enough funding to create a large multi-purpose and well-equipped space. Replicators may need to find ways to overcome shortcomings in both areas.

The Connected Learning Model May Provide an Overarching Theory that Can Guide Future Generations of YOUmedia-Like Initiatives

The Connected Learning Model, which drew on some findings of this study, was explicated as the study was drawing to a close. The model attempts to optimize learning by bringing together three spheres that are often disconnected in the lives of young people: interests, peer culture, and academic content. Many YOUmedia participants experience some parts of this model, although the Creators are most likely to experience all of the pieces. Teen interests and teen choice are central features at YOUmedia. In addition, social connections between teens and adults and among teens appear to be vibrant. YOUmedia is not as systematic about the linkages it is trying to promote between teens' experiences in the space and their academic lives. As YOUmedia builds on the Connected Learning framework, perhaps the associations will become more tangible between youths' interests and pursuits and academic achievement, career opportunities, and civic engagement.

YOUmedia accomplished much in its first three years. Relying on word of mouth and little or no additional outreach, it has been able to attract a large number of teens to its programs each week. It has proven to be highly adaptive to changing needs and teen interests. Being housed in the public library allows its benefits to be available at no charge to all Chicago residents, thereby mitigating the economic gap in access to such learning experiences. All participants are exposed to a variety of digital and traditional media opportunities in the context of a welcoming and safe environment. Such programs may well provide an example of the kinds of activities and philosophy that motivate and engage urban youth.

Endnotes

i   Ito, M., Gutierrez, K., Livingston, S., Penuel, W., Rhodes, J., Salen, K., Schor, J., Sefton-Green, J., and Watkins, S.C. (2013). *Connected Learning: An Agenda for Research and Design.* Irvine, CA: Digital Media and Learning Research Hub.

ii Ito, M., et al. (2009). *Hanging Out, Messing Around, and Geeking Out: Kids Living and Learning with New Media.* Cambridge, MA: MIT Press.

iii Fashiola, O.S. (2003). Developing the Talents of African American Male Students During the Nonschool Hours. *Urban Education, 38* (4): 398-430. Available online at http://uex.sagepub.com/content/38/4/398 (accessed on November 29, 2012).

Introduction

Brittany, wearing a shiny green butterfly ring and sunglasses, comes to the stage. She asks the crowd to please stand and clap while she sings; the instrumental for her song plays loudly over the speakers. The teens in the crowd clap in unison while she performs the song she recorded in the YOUmedia studio. The clapping stops briefly while she sings the chorus in a hushed tone: "I am, oh, I am, I am, much more than what you see."

Brittany participates in YOUmedia, a digital media-infused learning center for high school-aged youth at the Harold Washington Library Center (HWLC) in downtown Chicago. YOUmedia encompasses a physical space as well as a virtual place—a website—dedicated to YOUmedia users. Both are designed to draw youth into progressively more sophisticated levels of participation in digital and traditional media. Between 350 and 500 teens come to YOUmedia each week to hang out with their friends and work on projects. With the guidance of adult staff members, they can discover and pursue their interests through both collaborative and solitary activities, such as blogging, writing and sharing poetry, playing and reviewing electronic games, producing music and videos, and participating in book clubs. Special events open the door for youth to collaborate with and learn from recognized artists, authors, and experts. To understand teens' and adults' experiences and reactions to YOUmedia, the University of Chicago Consortium on Chicago School Research (UChicago CCSR), with the support of the John D. and Catherine T. MacArthur Foundation, conducted a three-year study to document the program and investigate whether and how it has fulfilled designers' aspirations.

Why Study Digital Media and Learning?

Digital media has special relevance for both out-of-school and in-school programs because it amplifies opportunities for learning. First, it can foster engagement and self-expression, as shown by Brittany's example. It was the digital recording studio at YOUmedia (along with support from staff) that allowed her to produce and perform her song. Other examples of digital tools that foster collaborative creation of products are Google Drive, blogs, and wikis. Second, digital media greatly increases the accessibility of information and learning experiences. They are literally at teens' fingertips, regardless of the device they use or whether they are at home, at school, or at a community center. This means that youth can access information and build knowledge that may not be available in their school or peer contexts. Third, digital media expands social supports for interests. Brittany could share her recording on YOUmedia Online (the closed social network) and receive comments and suggestions from her peers and staff. More generally, online communities have formed around a wide range of interests, and these communities allow individuals to share their creations and receive feedback and mentoring. Interacting with online communities not only allows delving into content but also supports building skills in collaboration and networking. Finally, digital media can play a role in expanding diversity and building community capacity. Forms of knowledge, culture, and values associated with non-dominant and marginalized communities are far more visible today and can be tapped for educational purposes.[2]

Given the opportunities that networked and digital media open up, it is not surprising that a tsunami of creative efforts is sweeping the country to exploit technology and digital media for instruction and learning. Whether it is blended learning (combining face-to-face instruction with technology-mediated activities), or iPads in schools, or video and music production in out-of-school settings, the landscape is chock-full of new products, curricula, approaches, and programs. An emerging market for educational entrepreneurs and the nearly universal adoption of the Common Core State Standards are opening up further opportunities to use technology for learning.[3]

At the same time, mastery of technological skills themselves now is considered so important that states and the federal government have begun to establish learning standards for them. The Common Core State Standards, which are currently being planned and implemented in schools across the country, call for technology use to be embedded in all aspects of students' learning.[4] In addition, the National Assessment of Educational Progress (NAEP) is now developing the first Technology and Engineering Literacy (TEL) Assessment, which will be administered in 2014. NAEP broadly defines technological and engineering literacy as the capacity to use, understand, and evaluate technology. The assessment will expect students to demonstrate skills in using technology to solve problems presented in realistic contexts and to communicate in a variety of ways, working both individually and in teams.[5]

Finally, policy makers are investing in technology and digital media for education. In 2010, as part of the "Educate to Innovate Campaign," President Obama announced a variety of public-private partnerships to promote science, technology, math, engineering, and digital media. One of these was the partnership between the MacArthur Foundation and the Institute of Museum and Library Services to fund the creation of 30 learning centers across the country modeled after YOUmedia. In his remarks, the President said that these initiatives advance his goal of empowering young people to be "makers and creators of things, rather than consumers."[6]

In the context of these opportunities, policies, and events, it is not surprising that there is great interest in and enthusiasm for innovative initiatives that build on the digital technologies. The question is whether such initiatives are on track to warrant such interest and enthusiasm. If not, in what ways should they change and adapt their models to better serve their purpose? Thus, what is needed is reliable evidence regarding on-the-ground initiatives with these digital media programs, the accomplishments and challenges of such initiatives, and recommendations for further design changes to more effectively facilitate opportunities for learning. This report documents the on-the-ground experiences of teens and adults with one such digital media initiative—YOUmedia at HWLC. It describes the youth who participate and categorizes and defines different types and levels of their participation; it highlights teens' perceptions about how they have grown and what they have learned. It also details the designers' initial aspirations and how these developed. And, it discusses the ways in which staff adapted to the complexities of an initiative that sought to build on teen interest by allowing them the free choice of whether or not to take part in activities intended to provide the skills necessary to advance that interest. Finally, it offers suggestions for strengthening YOUmedia Chicago and for establishing similar learning centers in other parts of the country.

YOUmedia Chicago: The Founders' Aspirations

We start by sharing what the founders of YOUmedia Chicago aspired for the teens who would come to and participate in YOUmedia. These were the leaders from the Chicago Public Library (CPL), the Digital Youth Network (DYN), and the MacArthur Foundation. These leaders' aspirations encompassed how youth would experience YOUmedia, what they would do in the space, and what skills and habits of mind they would acquire. Specifically the founders wanted YOUmedia to be a place where teens:

- Feel physically safe, free from danger, and emotionally safe; and are comfortable trying new activities
- Socialize with their peers
- Pursue their interests

- Develop competence in digital media
- Gain twenty-first century skills like communication, creativity, collaboration, and critical thinking
- Use books and library resources
- Produce artifacts
- Build their confidence
- Teach others
- Develop a sense of self-efficacy
- Create a community
- Understand college and career choices

With these goals at the forefront, YOUmedia opened in 2009 at the Harold Washington Library Center (HWLC) in downtown Chicago.

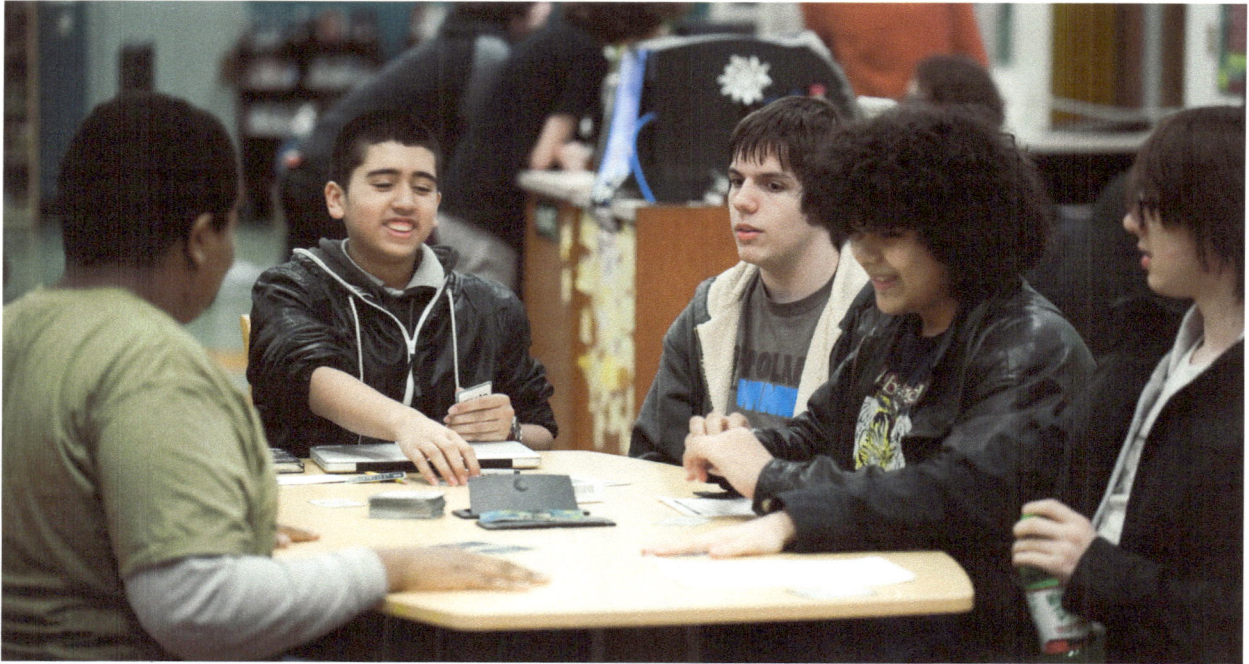

A Tour of YOUmedia Chicago

YOUmedia is conveniently located near an elevated train station and bus stops, making it readily accessible to thousands of Chicagoans. HWLC is the central library of a system of more than 70 locations in the City of Chicago.

At YOUmedia, there is no fee for teens with a library card to drop-in, hang out with friends, use the resources, and participate in learning activities. YOUmedia is open about 45 hours per week. It has a range of digital production equipment, from a sound studio to video and still cameras, to banks of computers equipped with video and photo editing software.

The designers of YOUmedia put teens' interests at the center of the space and program in an attempt to be "interest powered." Currently the programs center on music, spoken word, electronic gaming, writing, and design. The ten staff members are committed to constantly refreshing and adding new projects and workshops that appeal to adolescents' changing tastes. The program design also recognizes that teens' involvement in YOUmedia is driven by their friendships. The space invites hanging out with friends as well as collaborating with peers who have the same interests.

Staff often lead activities oriented to production and performance—songs, videos, a literature magazine, graphic designs, and poetry. These involve the most active teens, but the invitation is open to others too. Workshops provide training, and the online site showcases teens' and staff members' work. Teens are encouraged to reflect on their own and others' work and provide thoughtful critiques.

Because many teens also work on their school assignments at YOUmedia, the library recruited a certified high school teacher to be available for assistance.

Signature projects bring staff and the most active teens together to create shared productions. This includes weekly Lyricist Loft open mic (microphone) sessions, where teens perform poetry, music, and dance. Another is Chicago's biannual One Book, One Chicago program. Teens first read and discuss the book and then remix themes into poetry, stories, songs, or videos.

YOUmedia partners at times with other organizations, as it did with the Kennedy Center in Washington, D.C., to participate in What's Going On...Now. Teens at YOUmedia and in organizations in six other cities obtained access to the original sound tracks of Marvin Gaye's music. They wrote poetry, as well as created videos and multi-media presentations, about how the social conditions in the United States today mirror those of the early 1970s when Gaye produced his music.

YOUmedia at HWLC is the model for YOUmedia spaces established at four Chicago branch libraries for middle school-aged adolescents. In addition, YOUmedia is the model for 30 learning laboratories that are being launched in libraries and museums across the country.

YOUmedia Is an Innovative Approach

YOUmedia is a new combination of elements in a library that brings teens' social and learning worlds together.

If they are to succeed, educational innovations need several characteristics. They must be: informed by a scan of the wider environment; generated by able, informed practitioners; not officially sanctioned by education authorities, thus entailing risk; designed with an awareness of the strengths and weaknesses of conventional practice; user focused; and directed at helping to solve a serious modern problem.[7] In many ways, the creation of YOUmedia mirrored these characteristics. The MacArthur Foundation scanned the wider environment for ideas and possible partners before they decided which partnerships would be optimal and mutually beneficial. The Digital Youth Network (DYN) developed the YOUmedia program and curriculum in partnership with the Chicago Public Library (CPL) and with the support of the MacArthur Foundation and the Pearson Foundation. DYN is a group of academics, curriculum developers, and teaching artists (or informed practitioners) who drew on their experience in creating school-based and out-of school curricula in digital media literacy and mentoring youth to develop the learning activities at YOUmedia. Being user focused, the partners aimed to engage teens in creating, producing, and performing. They wanted to empower teens to become more expert in their areas of interest, thus giving them opportunities for learning beyond what they receive at school. As for HWLC, YOUmedia represented a radical change in library use by teens. Whereas teens had previously been an underserved population, YOUmedia provided them their own large space where they had access to library resources, digital production equipment, and, more importantly, opportunities for hands-on learning experiences.[8]

Research Base for YOUmedia

As we wrote in the year one report, *YOUmedia Chicago: Reimagining Learning, Literacies, and Libraries: A Snapshot of Year 1,*[9] YOUmedia was designed to promote three forms of digital media participation—"hanging out," "messing around," and "geeking out." These were identified through research conducted by Mimi Ito and her colleagues as the major ways adolescents interacted with new media. Hanging out is social participation with or around digital media. Teens socialize with their friends, check Facebook, and play video games. When messing around, teens show a budding interest in digital media and try out various practices that are often supported by the social networks they have established. Messing around is a transition zone between hanging out and geeking out. Teens who are geeking out display an intense commitment to media or technology, often developing advanced skills in a particular area like anime or gaming.[10] The physical space at YOUmedia incorporates zones for each of these participation types, and the designers originally expected that youth would progress from hanging out to messing around and then to geeking out.

After YOUmedia was launched and while the current UChicago CCSR study was underway, the Digital Media and Learning (DML) Hub at the University of California, Irvine, facilitated a process among MacArthur Foundation grantees and partners to generate a set of shared principles of learning and technology deployment that were emerging from their research and development. This approach was dubbed "Connected Learning." By YOUmedia's third year, its leaders and staff became familiar with Connected Learning as they attended conferences and worked with researchers and learning laboratories across the country. Although UChicago CCSR's study was not

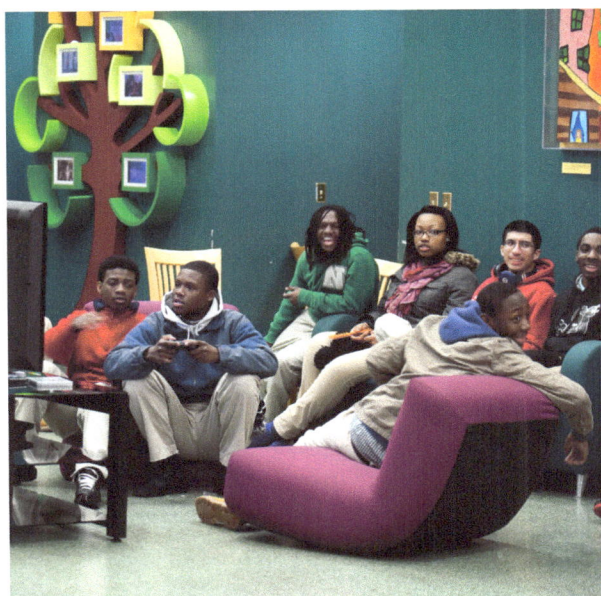

designed to measure elements of Connected Learning, by the end of the study there was sufficient interest in the model to warrant adding a few survey and protocol items relevant to it during final data collection activities. Thus, in Chapter 5, we discuss evidence we found of Connected Learning activities at YOUmedia.

Connected Learning occurs when a young person is able to follow a personal interest or passion with the support of peers and caring adults and can link this interest or learning to academic achievement, career success, or civic engagement. The model is based on evidence that the most effective learning occurs when the individual has a strong interest in the topic, has social support in pursuing the learning tasks, and receives recognition for accomplishments.[11]

Studying YOUmedia

Research on an Innovation

Studying an innovation requires a particular approach to asking questions, gathering evidence, and interpreting the results. This study most closely approximates "developmental evaluation," which is tailored to investigating social innovations. For these kinds of studies, the purpose is to gather evidence that can inform the development and further adaptation of the enterprise. This may require changing methods or measures midstream as the program theory and elements shift.[12] It also necessitates providing periodic feedback to the designers, staff, and funders. The fluid nature of developmental evaluation does not mean that any less evidence is brought to bear or that judgments are not made. Social innovators pursue their bold visions and plans, but researchers provide a steady stream of evidence on current realities. This means that the innovators must hold two distinct thought strands in their heads simultaneously: their visions for the future and the current reality on the ground.[13]

This Report Extends Previous Findings

The findings garnered during the first year of our research were documented in the report mentioned above, *YOUmedia Chicago: Reimagining Learning, Literacies, and Libraries*.[14] At the time, we explored the original theory of action for YOUmedia and contrasted that with what we observed during its first year in operation. The present report seeks to expand on those findings, bring to light new findings that were not yet available in our first year of research, and highlight where we have seen changes. Building on our first year report, we continued to track how the project evolved and to explore ways in which engagement in YOUmedia may have benefited the participants. Thus, the full answers to our research questions are cumulative and reflect what we learned during all three years of the study. **See sidebar *Highlights of Year One Report*** for a brief overview of the findings in our prior publication.

Research Questions

As is the nature with developmental evaluations, our research questions had to remain somewhat fluid as did our methods, and we adapted them as we learned more about the program. Nonetheless, we continuously attempted to answer whether YOUmedia was meeting the original aspirations of the designers. The questions are:

1. How is the program designed to engage youth in pursuing their interests?
2. Who are the youth who come to YOUmedia?
3. How do teens engage with YOUmedia?
4. Does YOUmedia offer a safe, welcoming place where teens have opportunities to pursue their interests?
5. What benefits do teens perceive from their participation in YOUmedia?
    (a) New and or expanded current interests?
    (b) New skills in digital and traditional media?
    (c) Greater expertise in an area of interest?
    (d) Expanded use of library resources?
    (e) Greater understanding of future college and career choices?
6. What roles does the staff play in introducing teens to resources, sparking their interests, and developing their skills?
7. How does staff adapt the program structures to facilitate youth engagement?
8. What challenges has YOUmedia faced in its initial years?

In UChicago CCSR's year one report on YOUmedia—which was intended to introduce YOUmedia to a wider community of those interested in digital media and youth development, including researchers, funders, and educators—we captured early experiences and assessed initial lessons. We determined how teens discovered YOUmedia and the variety of ways in which they interacted with the space. We identified obstacles encountered during YOUmedia's initial implementation (from fall 2009 through summer 2010) and examined programmatic responses to those challenges. We also examined what worked, identifying aspects of the program that were not initially anticipated to be useful but were found, in fact, to be necessary for ensuring effective use of digital media as an instrument for teens to learn critical skills.

The YOUmedia Partnership

Our first year report provided an overview of how YOUmedia came to be—the creation of partnerships facilitated by the MacArthur Foundation. With funding from the MacArthur Foundation Digital Media and Learning (DML) Initiative, YOUmedia intentionally combines the resources of the Chicago Public Library (CPL), which is a public institution committed to lifelong learning, and the Digital Youth Network (DYN), which is a digital media literacy program. Through a complex blend of each organization's knowledge and practices, YOUmedia provides a range of learning opportunities for youth.

The partnership between CPL and DYN has benefits for both organizations. While libraries possess a vast number of resources to support lifelong learning, digital media learning constitutes a foray into new terrain for CPL. DYN, however, offered a set of solutions for working with youth and digital media that broadened CPL's vision of what a library could be, particularly in attracting teens. The partnership also offered opportunities for DYN. A principal attraction to YOUmedia was that it provides an opportunity for DYN members to work through a more robust version of their existing model and apply it to a non-school setting.

A commitment to innovation required adaptations by all partners. The strategic partnership that was formed combined knowledge of public spaces, teen engagement, and design to create an innovative space. As this innovative vision began to take shape, all partners involved needed to depart from existing organizational paradigms and redefine their prior boundaries. New partnerships require that each institution meld into the broader vision.

For YOUmedia, this meant that members of CPL leadership had to examine several previously unquestioned policies about how patrons use the library. For DYN, these negotiations pushed them to reframe their traditional ideas of a digital media space and the role of adults in the space. In DYN's afterschool model, students participated in a session or class where an adult worked with them around a set of objectives; however, at the public library attendance is voluntary and participants are free to simply hang out. DYN staff were now charged with a different role.

Initial Theory of Action

The theory starts with youth gaining access to the physical space that is equipped with a range of digital production equipment. They also gain access to the online space. Both are embedded in a social environment. Together these elements provide opportunities for interest-driven interaction with adults serving as mentors and peers to use traditional and new media resources. Through participation, performances, and production of artifacts, teens are encouraged to acquire new expertise and confidence. YOUmedia was designed to be a new kind of environment that would encourage youth to move from a point of casual exploration of interests towards more serious and sustained engagement in new forms of learning.[15]

Key Findings

Our data collection, which included observations and interviews, resulted in four major findings about YOUmedia's first year of operation:

Relationships, particularly between youth and adult staff members, are crucially important in engaging teens toward productive growth. The initial theory of action for YOUmedia assumed that teens interacting with digital media tools and participating in activities centered on their interests would yield positive results around learning goals. During the first year, however, YOUmedia staff found that teens left on their own did not automatically connect their interests to workshops and other structured activities designed to teach them new skills and provide opportunities for them to explore interests more deeply. That changed when adults reached out to connect with youth socially and acted as guides and "cool" collaborators.

11

YOUmedia is cultivating a budding sense of community among teens who socialize and explore resources in the library. Peer relationships and an emerging sense of community serve as a potent force for driving teens to engage with digital technology in new ways. YOUmedia encourages teens to socialize, exchange ideas, and collaborate and share with their peers. Teens have come to view YOUmedia as a unique learning environment—one that does away with the formalities of high school and provides an environment where they feel free to explore their interests and express themselves.

Year one implementation created a dynamic learning environment for teens who participated. Flexibility among staff and fluid processes around programming has been shown to facilitate youth involvement at all participation levels. This flexibility is apparent when staff members shift away from an adult-structured model of teaching and activity design to one that is more closely tied to what

teens want to learn and how they want to learn it. Responsive formal learning opportunities—as well as informal, purposeful interactions—increase participation, expand social networks, and deepen teen under-standing and use of digital and traditional media.

Several challenges were evident in year one. As with all new organizations, YOUmedia faced some challenges in its first year. Organizationally it struggled with internal communication and role clarity, especially among part-time staff. In addition, like other activities based on voluntary participation, inconsistent teen attendance over time made it difficult to sustain coherence. Furthermore, while the online space was intended to motivate production and critique, it was not well utilized. Finally, resource availability and maintenance seem to be ongoing issues, from the choice of software utilization to the replacement and repair of equipment that is susceptible to breakage.

In pursuing these questions, we aim to provide a knowledge base that will be useful to the YOUmedia leaders at HWLC (and the four branch libraries with YOUmedias) in Chicago as they continue to adapt their model. This knowledge also is relevant to innovators who are currently designing and implementing learning laboratories based on YOUmedia Chicago in other institutions across the country.

Study Methods

To gauge the extent and nature of youth participation in YOUmedia, we administered two census questionnaires and two surveys. Because YOUmedia was not able to reliably track attendance, it was necessary to undertake two censuses to establish the characteristics of the YOUmedia population. The first census and survey took place in summer 2011. For the census, researchers were in the space during most of the hours YOUmedia was open in a single week. They approached every teen and asked five background questions. The following week, researchers returned to invite teens to participate in an online survey, offering them a $5 gift certificate for a sandwich shop. The characteristics of the survey group

were similar to those of the census. In spring 2012, the same procedures were again used to conduct a census and survey. (**See Appendix A** for full details.)

Most of the questions on the anonymous surveys were about participants' experiences at YOUmedia: when they began coming and how much time they spend there; what they do at YOUmedia; whether it is a comfortable environment; whether they pursue new/existing interests; whether they collaborate with adult staff and other teens; and what benefits, if any, they receive from participation.

To gain a deeper understanding of the diverse experiences of youth at YOUmedia, we selected 23 teens for in-depth case studies and interviewed them three times during a 15-month period, using a semi-structured interview protocol. Recommended by the staff, these youth reflected a broad range of participation and engagement levels in the program, as well as a range of background characteristics.

To investigate the perceptions, experiences, and concerns of the staff, researchers interviewed ten staff members—both DYN and library personnel—on four different occasions during the study. At three different time points, researchers also interviewed the founders and leaders of YOUmedia, including leaders at DYN, CPL, and the MacArthur Foundation.

Finally, researchers spent considerable time in the space observing teens' and staff members' activities and interactions. One researcher was "embedded" at YOUmedia (present at least half time) for about 18 months.

Overview of the Report

In Chapter 1, *The Hybrid Design of YOUmedia*, we examine the origins of YOUmedia—the research antecedents and the partnership between CPL and the DYN. Prior research pointed the program planners toward a hybrid design, and the respective cultures of the partnering organizations reinforced the roles of both unstructured and structured learning activities.

In Chapter 2, *Teens at YOUmedia and Their Participation*, we introduce the YOUmedia teens, including where they live, the schools they attend, and the considerable distance that most of them travel to be a part of YOUmedia. We also detail basic demographic characteristics and compare their use of technology to that of the overall CPS high school population. We analyze what teens do when they come to YOUmedia in the context of a hybrid design that allows teens to make choices about how to participate. Five general types of YOUmedia participation are illustrated: Socializers, Readers/Studiers, Floaters, Experimenters, and Creators.

Teens' reactions to the space are explored in Chapter 3, *Benefits of YOUmedia*. We analyze how teens take ownership of YOUmedia and develop, along with the staff, a safe, welcoming community. Finally we share youth perceptions on the benefits they perceive from participating in YOUmedia: improvements in digital media skills, academic skills, and greater understanding of future college and career opportunities.

Chapter 4, *Adult Support, Teen Choice, and Program Challenges*, focuses on the impact of the hybrid design on key program elements: the important mentoring role played by the staff; learning activities; and YOUmedia Online, the closed social network. Considering the high degree of teen choice at YOUmedia, the adults play a critical role as the conduit between teens' interests and learning activities and projects. At the same time, it is challenging for staff to balance the multiple—and at times competing—needs of the youth participants, from those who primarily socialize to those who study to those who record music or perform poetry. This chapter compares the efficacy of workshops and projects and discusses the functions of YOUmedia Online.

In the final chapter, *Interpretive Summary and Considerations for Practice*, we discuss lessons for the future for both YOUmedia Chicago and other similar learning laboratories. In addition, we examine the implications of the findings for creating environments that promote Connected Learning.[16]

The Hybrid Design of YOUmedia

The leaders and staff at YOUmedia recognized at the outset that YOUmedia could serve as a source of learning that complements learning at school, in the community, and in the family. Thus, they saw YOUmedia as one node in a teen's learning ecology. They posited that students would build on an existing interest or develop a new interest. They would gain more expertise through exposure to learning opportunities and accessible role models—both adult and peer—that would scaffold those opportunities and encourage increased interest and skill. The space was intentionally a "hybrid"; it was designed to offer unstructured opportunities for teens to hang out and socialize with friends, space for casual experimentation with digital tools, and more structured learning experiences through workshops and special events.

Research on out-of-school time (OST) generally supports the point of view that well-implemented OST programs can provide such learning experiences; other benefits can include higher rates of school attendance and improved academic achievement.[17] OST programs can also boost social, career, and civic skills for older youth if they have opportunities for team-building work and for developing strong relationship with adults.[18] Integrating digital media into the out-of-school environment provides further advantages in that it may help to link home, school, community, and peer contexts, and it may facilitate youth working with each other and adults on projects in which they have a shared interest. Such activities can occur anywhere and anytime.[19] A young person who is creating a video at home, school, or an out-of-school setting can consult with adult mentors or teachers online to get advice.

In this chapter, we focus on how YOUmedia was structured as an out-of-school program. We describe the overall design and the key program structures of YOUmedia—the staff, learning activities, and closed social network. The program designers established these structures to encourage teens to pursue their interests and to promote the learning of skills—both digital media skills and more general twenty-first century skills (e.g., communication, creativity, and collaboration, which was mentioned earlier). As YOUmedia developed, staff roles and program structures evolved over time as we will describe. This chapter provides context for subsequent chapters about what teens do at YOUmedia.

CHAPTER 1 ADDRESSES THE FOLLOWING QUESTION:

How is the program designed to engage youth in pursuing their interests?

YOUmedia Is a Hybrid

Based on our observations and interviews in the space, we found YOUmedia to be a combination of distinctly different components. It contains elements not only of an unstructured public space but also of a structured out-of-school program. **Figure 1** elaborates the differences between these two components. In an unstructured drop-in space (e.g., an open gym at a YMCA), teens can choose when they come to the space and what they do while they are there. There may be adults supervising, but the activities are not formally organized. In a structured out-of-school program, however, adults develop much of the agenda, organize formal activities, establish goals, and provide mentoring to teens; typically staff members also establish some forms of communication with parents. In addition to an open gym, a YMCA may offer structured activities (e.g., basketball, soccer, swimming, theater productions, or community projects). In this regard, YOUmedia may be similar to a YMCA in that it offers both structured and unstructured activities. What is distinct about YOUmedia, however, is how the combination is manifested; it is a particular combination of unstructured and structured

15

FIGURE 1

YOUmedia combines unstructured and structured elements

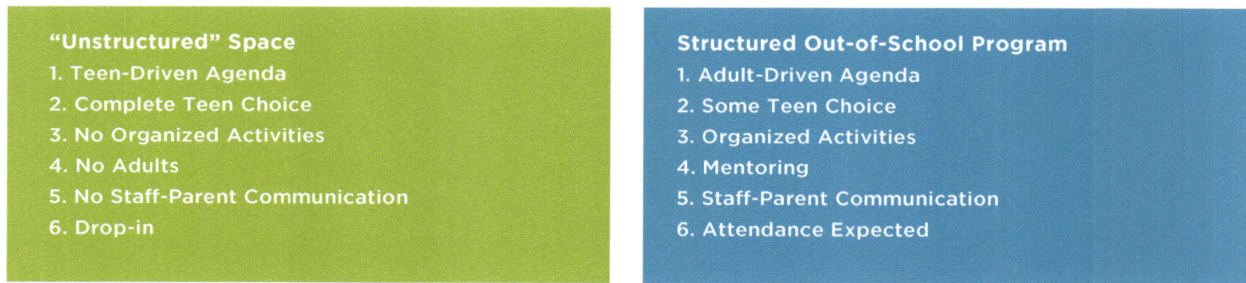

"Unstructured" Space	Structured Out-of-School Program
1. Teen-Driven Agenda	1. Adult-Driven Agenda
2. Complete Teen Choice	2. Some Teen Choice
3. No Organized Activities	3. Organized Activities
4. No Adults	4. Mentoring
5. No Staff-Parent Communication	5. Staff-Parent Communication
6. Drop-in	6. Attendance Expected

YOUmedia

activities all in the same space and at the same time. Adult staff members work as mentors and create formal opportunities for learning and skill development, but teens who choose to come to the space are free to engage in these organized activities, pursue other interests supported in the space, or just relax. More importantly, they can easily go back and forth between structured and unstructured activities. For example, they may hang out for a while, sit in on a workshop on spoken word, write a poem, post the poem on a social network, and then chat with friends online about the poem. One of the friends may suggest a particular "app" to enhance the poem, which leads the writer to download and use the app. Thus, youth at YOUmedia can move fluidly between structured and unstructured activities.

Figure 2 characterizes where the program falls along certain dimensions between unstructured and structured out-of-school programs. While the figure is not intended to convey the numeric precision of a scale, it does highlight the unique combination of features. Note that YOUmedia balances a teen-driven agenda with an adult-driven agenda. It also tilts toward both teen choice and adult mentoring. This means that teens have the autonomy of choice in a context where the adults play significant roles in teaching, advising, and coaching. As we will see later on in this report, a special dynamic is set up between the adults and the youth. Staff members who are effective in mentoring teens are likely to negotiate with, nudge, and cajole them.

The hybrid design of YOUmedia derives in part from the founders' decision to put into practice the seminal

ethnographic research conducted by Mimi Ito and her colleagues. Her research found that the most common behaviors teens exhibit around digital media are hanging out, messing around, and geeking out.[20] It was the plan of the founders of YOUmedia to provide physical spaces for all three activities, though they are not sharply delineated. The hanging out area has comfortable furniture where teens can socialize, check Facebook, play games, and browse through the library's young adult book collection. The messing around area is identified by red flooring and also has a gaming console, comfortable seating, reference materials, and kiosks with PC and Mac desktop computers. A studio provides tools to produce music and other audio recordings. The geeking out area is designed as a more serious work space. It is located far from the chatter of the hanging out space and features moveable conference tables, dry erase boards, and a SMART board. Here teens can use laptops, cameras, and other digital equipment to make digital media products.[21]

The hybrid design of YOUmedia also stems from the initial partnership that established the program. In our year one report, we detailed the collaborative efforts that made the creation of YOUmedia possible. The Chicago Public Library (CPL) and the Digital Youth Network (DYN) launched and operated YOUmedia together. Each organization has its own distinct mission and culture. CPL seeks to provide "all Chicagoans with a free and open place to gather, learn, connect, read and be transformed."[22] DYN promotes "access and training in the use of new media literacy tools and meaningful

FIGURE 2

YOUmedia is a particular combination of unstructured and structured features

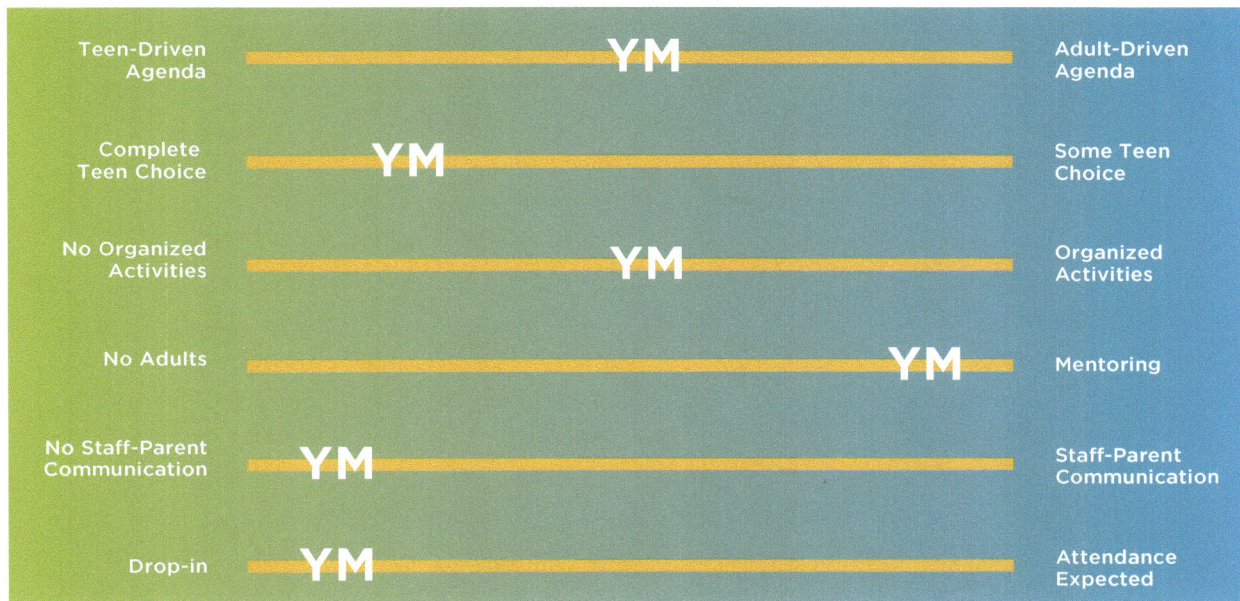

Teen-Driven Agenda		Adult-Driven Agenda
Complete Teen Choice		Some Teen Choice
No Organized Activities		Organized Activities
No Adults		Mentoring
No Staff-Parent Communication		Staff-Parent Communication
Drop-in		Attendance Expected

activities...to help teens develop new media literacies and critical thinking skills...to become engaged citizens in their communities."[23] These differences affected the design and operation of YOUmedia. This will be discussed in greater detail in Chapter 4.

The degree of teen choice that YOUmedia offers is noteworthy and has a profound effect on how teens interact with the program, as we will detail in Chapter 2. Interviews with teens revealed that choice seems to set YOUmedia apart from many other out-of-school options. Indeed, teens have a wealth of out-of-school activities in which they can get involved, including school-based clubs, recreational and competitive sports teams, and community-based programs. But, teens report that YOUmedia is different than these other places they can go after school. One of the boys who participated in the literary programs at YOUmedia explained:

> I don't know other places that I'd go to... that aren't pushing some mission on you, like, "Let's save the youth of our urban communities." I'm sure YOUmedia has that as one of their goals, but they're not forcing it down your throat.

Program Structures that Evolved and Became Constant

DYN and CPL Staff Members

Both DYN and CPL contribute staff members to YOUmedia. DYN and CPL staff teach workshops and mentor teens through the process of exploring and pursuing current and new interests. The library staff also manage various aspects of YOUmedia operations, and develop or assist with programs. Like the DYN staff, several had prior experience working in learning environments with youth and have personal interests in digital media. DYN staff also have a range of professional expertise in traditional and digital mediums, including poetry, editorial writing, electronic music production, graphic design, and analog art (drawing).

Initially, DYN and CPL staff differed in their approaches to engaging teens. Librarians, based on their traditional role of providing resources to patrons, did not take on a direct role in teaching or mentoring, whereas the DYN staff had been hired specifically to carry out these roles. In the early stages of YOUmedia's development, the two groups began meeting regularly to develop a common knowledge base and shared set of practices for performing the mentor and teaching role as librarians began to take on some of these responsibilities. This has brought greater, though not complete, alignment. Nonetheless, today the roles have become more fixed, with the expectation that both librarians and DYN staff have teaching and mentoring responsibilities. This change in role represents a departure from the typical role of a librarian and is a byproduct of a fluid and dynamic space that is constantly adapting to meet the socio-emotional and learning needs of youth who attend YOUmedia. To the youth, the fact that staff members are employed by separate organizations is not evident; they view all adult staff as mentors.

Formal Learning Activities

In YOUmedia's first year, the staff was intent on creating rules and routines to ensure that tools and equipment remained functional. They were also particularly intentional about maintaining safety at YOUmedia—creating not only a safe place for teens to be creative but also a space where people and their property were treated with respect. Staff also designed workshops and other activities around teens' interests in an attempt to move teens from casual use and consumption of digital media to creating digital products. The staff continually experimented with different approaches and engaged in trial and error in selecting different content areas to appeal to the teens, who had the choice of signing up for a workshop or not.[24]

During years two and three, the program continued to evolve as YOUmedia staff experimented with the design and content of structured learning activities. However, a number of programs are now fixed offerings based on the consistent engagement and participation of the teens. More training in the use of the sound studio and a certification system prepares the teens to use the expensive equipment. Teens perform poetry, music, and dance at a weekly open mic session. One Book, One Chicago is a constant. Free programming is offered throughout the city related to a book that is selected twice annually. YOUmedia staff organize youth book discussion groups; invite authors to give readings and discussions; and ask teens to create their own work inspired by the book (e.g., poetry, short stories, videos, or songs).

Workshops also changed. Initially, they tended to be curriculum-based, emphasizing the goal of skill development through sequential and cumulative learning objectives. Eventually the staff created project-based workshops to support special events with external partners, and more recently they have developed theme-based workshops that are one- or two-session demonstrations designed to pique teens' curiosity about the creative possibilities of a particular digital medium.

In part, the change in workshops reflects adults' shifting learning goals. Originally they worked to move teens along a continuum of hanging out to messing around to geeking out. The focus has gradually shifted to training or "leveling up" the most active teens to prepare them for opportunities that arise from robust partnerships with noteworthy organizations, including the Kennedy Center, the Museum for Contemporary Art, and Lady Gaga's Born This Way Foundation.[25] The teens need training and experience to effectively create digital media artifacts as part of these larger projects or competitions. In Chapter 4, we elaborate on these changes in greater detail.

YOUmedia Online

In addition to the physical space at HWLC, YOUmedia also exists as an online space. Because it is a closed social networking site, users must be involved with YOUmedia and sign up to participate. Like other social networks, the online space allows teens to create personal pages, join online groups based upon interests or in connection with workshops in the physical space, post and comment on media, and message their peers. (The site also permits teens to directly link to Facebook and Tumblr.) Yet the YOUmedia online space differs from many popular social networking sites in its inclusion of explicit pedagogical and motivational purposes. In addition to providing an opportunity for social networking amongst the teens who engage at YOUmedia, the online space is intended to promote learning using incentives and feedback from both peers and adults.[26] The hybrid nature of YOUmedia is mirrored by this inclusion of both social networking activity and learning activities that are focused on digital media production.

But after two years, teens were discouraged from using the social network by major changes. YOUmedia joined the Chicago Hive Learning Network, a group of youth-serving organizations that engage youth based on their interests and often make use of digital media and mentors. This resulted in multiple additional organizations gaining access to the site. Almost simultaneously the platform was upgraded, and the management of the site changed. The site looked different to the users, and there were many other teens on the site who did not attend YOUmedia at HWLC. We detail these events in Chapter 3 and explain how the thinking has evolved on the best uses for the social network.

In summary, YOUmedia seeks to encourage youth to pursue their interests by offering an extensive menu of possibilities. These include a richly equipped, comfortable physical space where teens can socialize and/or pursue their interests; staff members who mentor and teach; workshops; projects; a closed social network; and high profile special events. In essence, YOUmedia bridges teens' social and learning worlds. Next we explore how teens approach these choices.

19

CHAPTER 2

Teens at YOUmedia and Their Participation

IN THIS CHAPTER, WE ADDRESS TWO QUESTIONS:

Who are the youth who come to YOUmedia?
How do teens engage with YOUmedia?

By choosing to establish the first YOUmedia program in Chicago in the city's main library, the founders were clearly focused on reaching out to urban youth and providing them with innovative and engaging learning experiences beyond what they receive at school. In this chapter, we introduce and describe the teens who visit YOUmedia, including their basic demographic characteristics, where they live, the schools they attend, how they travel to YOUmedia, and their use of technology. We also analyze and detail the variety of ways teens participate in YOUmedia.

As noted before, we estimate that during most weeks 350 to 500 unique teens visit YOUmedia at the Harold Washington Library Center (HWLC). The teens who visit YOUmedia come from all across the city; they represent over 50 different high schools and are likely to live at least five miles from HWLC. Because most of the youth coming to YOUmedia heard about it through word of mouth, extensive outreach or marketing was not necessary.

Through our surveys, we learned that YOUmedia teens typically have experience using digital media prior to their first visit and believe they are more competent using technology than their peers. Because the physical space is designed to allow teens to choose what they do at YOUmedia, there are different levels and patterns of participation. We describe five types of participants derived from these usage patterns: Socializers, Readers/Studiers, Floaters, Experimenters, and Creators.

YOUmedia's Teens Are Heterogeneous but Differ from the CPS High School Population

Most Teens Are African American, with the Largest Single Group being African American Males

YOUmedia at HWLC has successfully attracted African American youth. Most (66 percent) of the teens who visit YOUmedia describe themselves as African American, which is higher than the percentage of the CPS high school population (46 percent). On the other hand, the portion of those who describe themselves as Latino/a (12 percent) is smaller than the percentage of the CPS high school population (41 percent). CPL recently opened YOUmedias for middle school-aged children in four branch libraries, including the Humboldt Park and Lozano Branches that serve the Puerto Rican and Mexican communities, respectively (**see Appendix C**). Hence, while YOUmedia at HWLC may not serve as many Latino/a youth, this population is targeted at other branches.

The biggest single group is African American males, who are 40 percent of YOUmedia's teens (**see Table 1**). This is almost twice as much as the CPS high school population (22 percent). A large fraction of these males come to YOUmedia to record and produce music in the sound studio. Given that African American males historically have been underserved by schools and out-of-school programs,[27] YOUmedia has developed a successful strategy for attracting users and for keeping them coming back for more visits.

TABLE 1

Percent of YOUmedia teens in each category

	African American	Latino/a	White	Asian/PI	Other	Total
Age						
15/younger	9	2	2	0	2	15
16-17	40	7	5	2	6	60
18/older	17	2	0	0	6	25
Gender						
Female	26	3	2	0	5	36
Male	40	8	5	2	9	64
Total	66	11	7	2	14	100

Source: 2012 YOUmedia Survey

YOUmedia Teens Are More Likely to Attend a Selective Enrollment High School than CPS Students Overall

Most YOUmedia teens (88 percent) attend a CPS high school, and they come from 50 different schools. Others are either homeschooled (3 percent), attend a private high school (2 percent), attend a suburban high school (2 percent), or do not identify their school (5 percent). The homeschooled teens visit YOUmedia once a week to work with a staff member to create multimedia or other projects inspired by a book they have read.

YOUmedia teens who attend a CPS high school are over three times more likely to attend a selective enrollment high school than the CPS high school student population (35 versus 10 percent). This is notable because selective enrollment schools are more likely than other CPS high schools to provide students with a technologically rich educational experience[28] and students attending them are among the highest-achieving youth in the city. In addition, YOUmedia youth are more likely than other CPS students to attend a military academy (12 versus 2 percent). They are equally as likely as other CPS students to attend a charter school.

FIGURE 3

Teens who attend YOUmedia are more likely to attend selective enrollment high schools than the CPS high school population

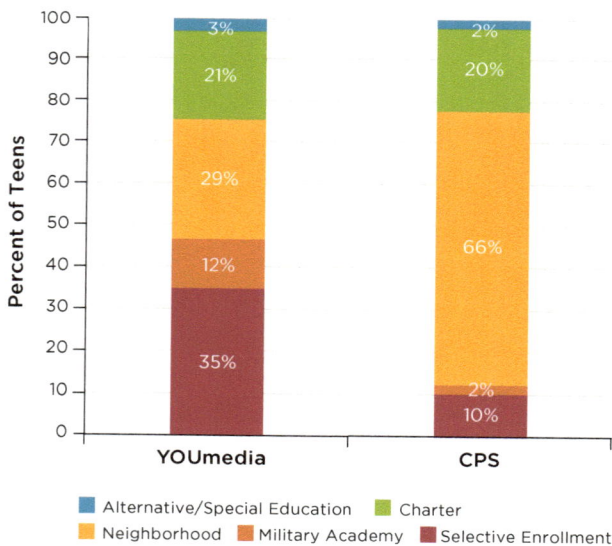

Source: 2012 YOUmedia Survey

Note: Selective enrollment high schools offer academically rigorous curricula and have highly competitive application processes. Military academies focus on leadership skills and military training and require students to meet a minimum academic standard. Neighborhood high schools have open enrollment policies that generally serve all students who live within a given attendance area. Charter high schools, which require an application, are public schools that are independently operated but not subject to the same state laws and policies as traditional public schools. Alternative high schools serve teens removed from other schools for behavioral violations. Special education high schools provide students with disabilities with an individualized education.

YOUmedia Teens Reside throughout Chicago but Are More Concentrated in the South/Southeast Sides

Teens come from all parts of Chicago, and nearly 80 percent live more than five miles from HWLC (**see Figure 4 and Appendix B**). More than half, 54 percent, live either south or southeast, which is greater than for CPS overall (29 percent). Eighteen percent of YOUmedia teens live either north or northwest—half the CPS rate (36 percent). Another 18 percent of YOUmedia teens live southwest, compared to 29 percent of CPS students (**Appendix C** contains supplementary tables).

FIGURE 4
Home zip codes of YOUmedia teens

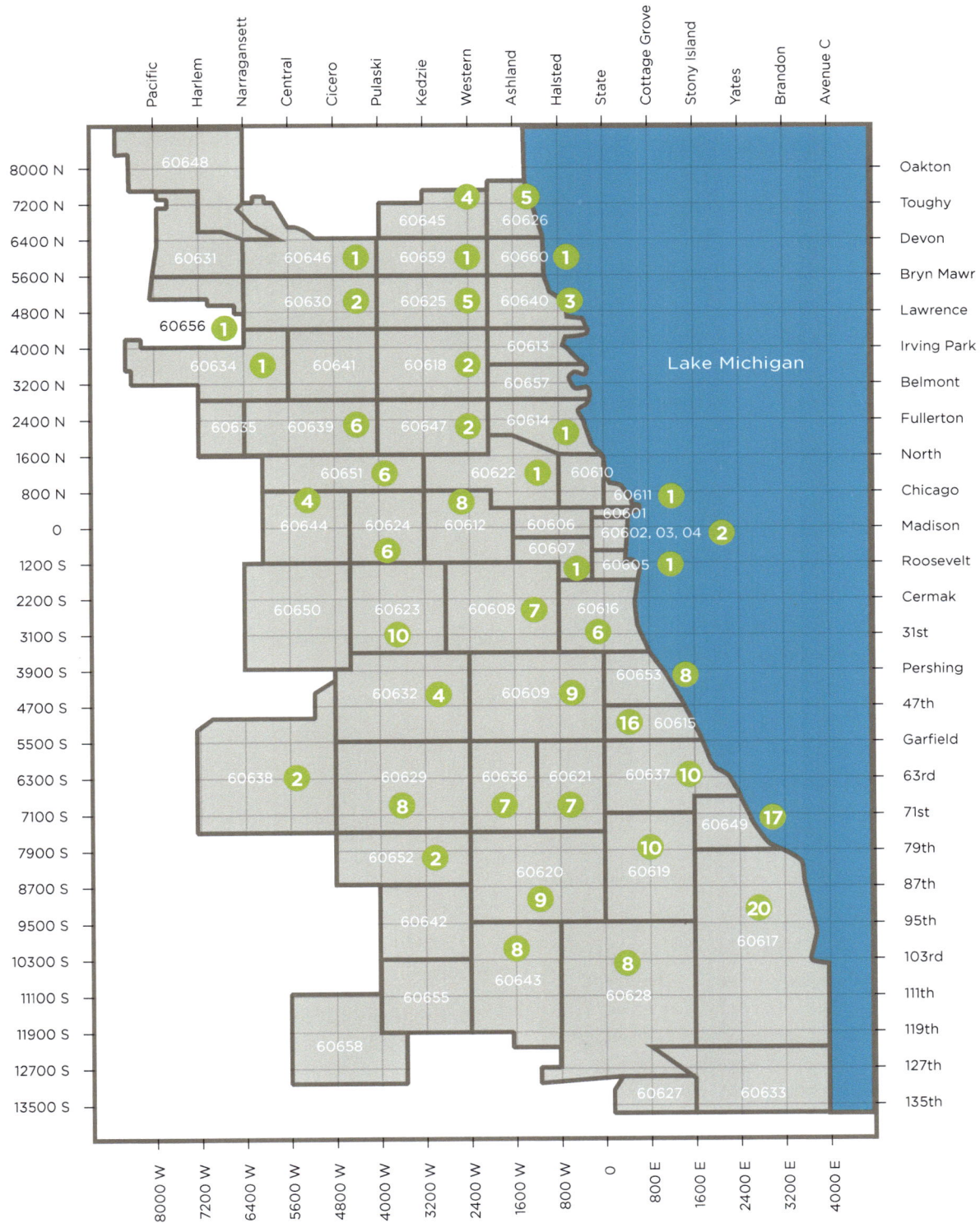

Number of youth from each area. Teens from suburbs not shown.

YOUmedia Teens' Families Are Heterogeneous

To gain some understanding of the social and economic background of the teens' families, we asked them about their mother's highest education level. This is often used as a proxy in the social sciences for socio-economic conditions. We found that the YOUmedia teens come from a heterogeneous group of families. Thirty-eight percent of YOUmedia teens report that their mothers have a four-year college degree. Among the rest of the teens, 25 percent say their mothers have some college or two-year degree; 26 percent indicate that their mothers have a high school diploma; and 4 percent say their mothers have less than a high school diploma; another 6 percent of teens in our sample did not know their mother's educational attainment (see Appendix C).

Half of YOUmedia Teens Make Considerable Effort to Visit HWLC

YOUmedia's central downtown location, near "L" subway stations and bus stops, facilitates access for teens. About half of the YOUmedia teens make a considerable commitment of time and expense to visit YOUmedia. For the rest, there may be a little less effort because they either go to school nearby or stop at YOUmedia on their way home from school.

Given that so many teens live so far away, we thought it important to understand their travel patterns. Knowing the zip code of their homes, the schools they attend, and the nearest public transportation option for each, we identified three dominant travel patterns.

- **Downtown Anyway.** Twenty-five percent of YOUmedia teens either attend school or live in close proximity to HWLC. A large majority (84 percent) of this group attend school close by. Easy access to YOUmedia may encourage them to take advantage of it. Even though their school is nearby, most of them still live in faraway neighborhoods throughout the city.

- **On the Way Home from School.** Twenty-five percent of YOUmedia teens stop on their way home from school. These youth attend schools throughout the city and have to travel through downtown to get home. Like the "Downtown Anyway" group, convenience makes it easy for them to get to YOUmedia.

- **Special Trip.** Fifty percent of YOUmedia teens make a special trip to HWLC. These teens do not attend school or live nearby, and HWLC is not on their way home from school. They have the longest travel times and the most expense.

What is apparent from this analysis of travel patterns is how convenient YOUmedia is for teens coming from many sections of Chicago. As Learning Laboratories are established in this city and others, location will be a critical factor.

Most YOUmedia Teens Have High Speed Internet at Home—Same as CPS Average

Percent with High Speed Internet:	
YOUmedia Teens	74%
CPS HS Students	76%

Source: 2012 UChicago CCSR Student Survey

Most YOUmedia Teens Think They Are Better than Their Peers at Using Technology

When planning YOUmedia, the founders knew that a high proportion of families with children had computers at home and that most high school-aged youth had experience with them. But YOUmedia would provide a wider range of equipment and software as well as adults who could teach and provide guidance. What the founders could not predict was the skill levels of the teens who come to YOUmedia. We included items on our survey instruments to capture this information.

Many of the teens reported that, even before coming to YOUmedia, they were actively using and producing artifacts with digital media:

- More than one half posted original work online and gave feedback on someone else's digital project.

- Close to one-half revised a posting based on feedback.

- About one-third created a blog post, an original video game, or a song; they used multiple types of media to create their product.

- About one-fourth created an original song or video and created an original graphic design. (**See Appendix C** for full details.)

When asked about how they compare to their peers in using technology, most teens—two-thirds—told us they are better than their peers (**see Figure 5**). This may reflect their prior experience and attendance at YouMedia.

FIGURE 5

YOUmedia teens comparing themselves to their peers in using technology

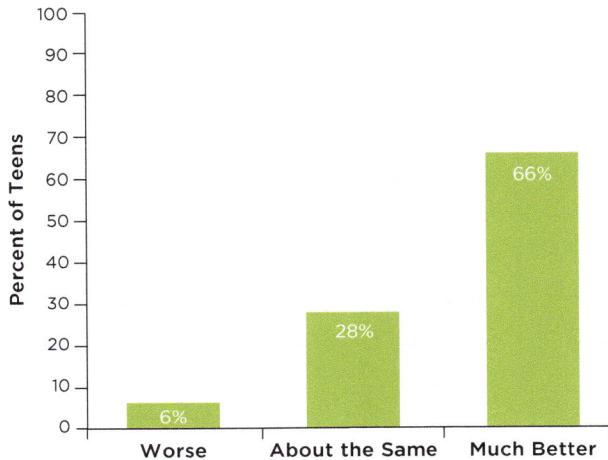

Source: 2012 YOUmedia Survey

Teens Visit YOUmedia Frequently and Consistently

We turn now to what the teens do at YOUmedia starting with basic attendance. It is challenging for out-of-school programs geared to teens to persuade them to visit for the first time and then to keep them coming back over time. According to research on out-of-school programs, this challenge is greater for teens than for younger students because teens frequently participate in other activities, have other responsibilities like jobs or family obligations, and/or can choose how they spend their time.[29]

Although YOUmedia has no attendance requirements, it has been successful at attracting and retaining teens over time. On our spring 2012 survey, we asked teens how long and often they visit YOUmedia (**see Figure 6**). Half the teens reported that they had been visiting the space for more than a year, and almost two-thirds (24 percent plus 39 percent) indicated visiting YOUmedia at least once a week during a year. Over one-third (39 percent) of teens reported attending both weekly and for more than one year.

FIGURE 6

Duration and frequency of teen attendance

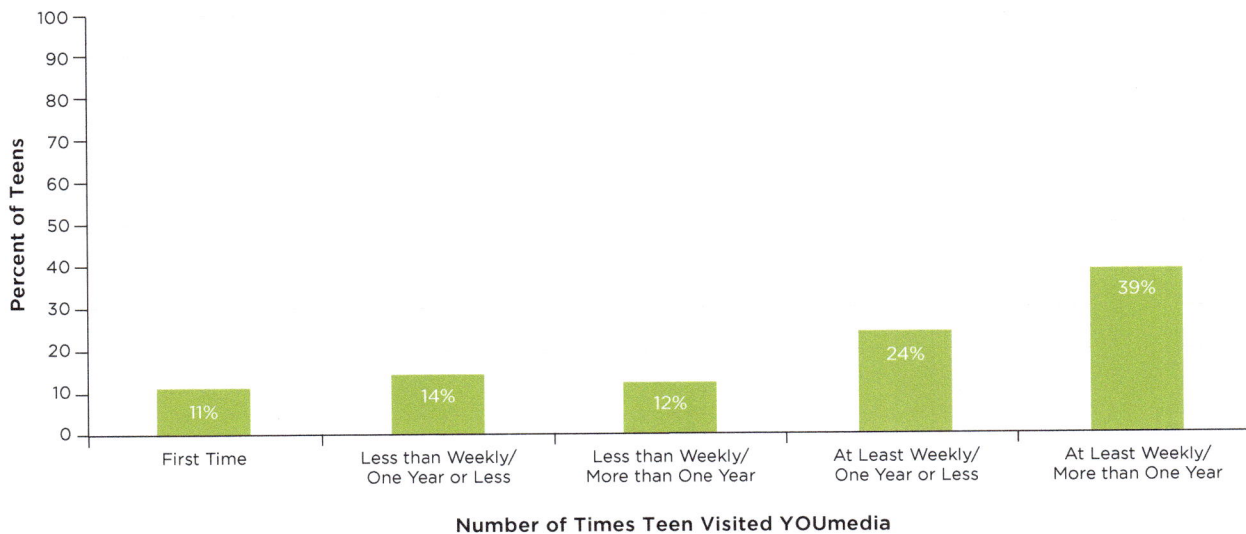

Source: 2012 YOUmedia Survey

Teen Choice Provides Diverse Opportunities for Participation

To understand how teens participate in YOUmedia at HWLC, we synthesized data gathered from the site visits and surveys. An item on the spring 2012 survey asked teens to describe what they spend most of their time doing when at YOUmedia. Combining this information with observations and interviews revealed five broad patterns or types of teen participation at YOUmedia. These types reflect varying levels of attendance, involvement in workshops, use of equipment, interaction with staff and participation in creation activities. We designated the five types of participation as Socializer, Reader/Studier, Floater, Experimenter, and Creator.

Socializers hang out with friends, attend open mic sessions, and/or play card or board games. Readers/Studiers do homework, check out books, and/or read.

Floaters use the computers, and/or play video games. Experimenters use the equipment, mostly sitting down at a keyboard or computer to play music. Creators reserve the recording studio to produce their music, work with an adult on projects like YOUlit magazine or a Library of Games podcast, or work on art projects.

Figure 7 displays the types of participation and the percentages of teens who represent each one during the time of the 2012 survey administration.

It is important to note that we consider the categorization of an individual teen as a snapshot of how he or she described himself or herself in spring 2012. A teen's type may change over time as involvement with YOUmedia ebbs and flows according to personal interests and the offerings of YOUmedia.

We discuss each participation type below (**see Appendix C** for survey responses for each participation type).

FIGURE 7

Types of teen participation

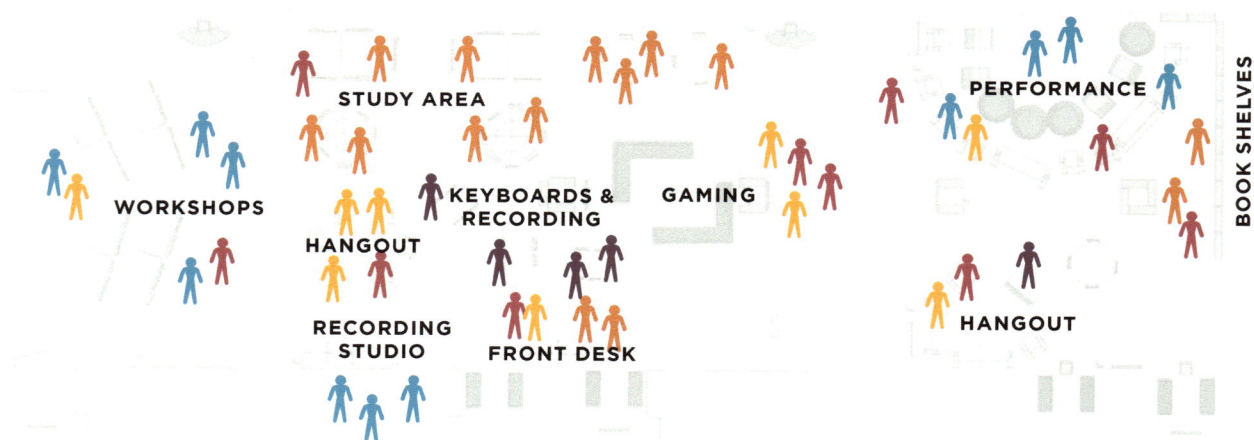

Socializer, 18%: found throughout the space chatting with friends and staff, playing board games, and attending open mic performances.

Reader/Studier, 28%: found browsing YOUmedia's library stacks, talking with librarians about books, reading, and working on schoolwork.

Floater, 21%: play video games, use the computers, hang out with friends, and attend open mic; they are likely to do many of these things on a single visit. Floaters are playing games, watching a movie or YouTube, checking Facebook or email, surfing the web, and/or doing their homework.

Experimenter, 11%: mainly interested in music. Instead of using the music studio, they take advantage of the computers and keyboards to practice and write music. They often chat or work with friends, but they rarely interact with the staff.

Creator, 22%: create music in the studio, work on art and graphic design projects, create podcasts, blogging, and writing and performing poetry.

Note: Each figure represents two students. The placement of the figures demonstrates where students tend to congregate.

Socializers

Socializers visit YOUmedia to spend time with their friends. They are found throughout the space chatting with friends and staff, playing board games, and attending open mic performances. Most Socializers have visited YOUmedia for at least a year and most visited at least weekly. More than half of the Socializers are female, and one-third attend a selective enrollment high school. Most Socializers are long-term regular visitors to YOUmedia. Almost two-thirds have been introduced to a new interest, and about one-third have attended a workshop.

TASHA: A YOUmedia Socializer

Participation at YOUmedia: Tasha learned about YOUmedia from her friends. She is a YOUmedia veteran who has been visiting the space for more than 1.5 years. Her visits are frequent and usually last for about an hour. Tasha considers YOUmedia to be a space to "chill" with her friends and use the computer to surf the internet. She and her friends often use a computer together, getting on Facebook or taking pictures with the Photobooth application. She is aware that various programs are available at YOUmedia but has never wanted to participate because she is involved in so many other afterschool activities, including the debate team, student government, school band, sports, volunteering, and After School Matters (a local out-of-school program). For her, YOUmedia is just a fun place to meet up and hang out with friends. In her words, "I just thought...the place was...really fun...I'd never known for the library to be, you know, fun for teenagers. I thought it was just all books." Although she does not participate in workshops, she occasionally attends showcases and other special events to see other teens perform their work.

Relationship with Staff: Even though she has not attended workshops, Tasha has strong relationships with the adult staff at YOUmedia. She says that among her favorite aspects of YOUmedia is the staff, including the security guards. She feels she can trust the staff and says she relates better to them than to other adults in her life.

Benefits of YOUmedia: While Tasha has not been involved with digital media production at YOUmedia, she does report gaining benefits from the program. She feels YOUmedia has helped with her writing skills, schoolwork, and ability to communicate with teachers and other adults. She says that coming to YOUmedia has helped her learn how to better use computers, specifically Apple computers that were unfamiliar to her.

Readers/Studiers

Readers/studiers visit YOUmedia for the same reasons other teens visit traditional libraries—to look for and check out books and to do their schoolwork. They are found browsing YOUmedia's library stacks, talking with librarians about books, reading, and working on schoolwork (sometimes, but not always, on a computer). More than half of Readers/Studiers have visited for at least a year, and more than half have visited at least weekly. More than half of Readers/Studiers are male, and one-third attend a selective enrollment high school. Most Readers/Studiers are long-term regular visitors to YOUmedia and report being introduced to a new interest; less than half (43 percent) participate in YOUmedia's workshops.

KAYLA: A YOUmedia Reader/Studier

Participation at YOUmedia: Kayla first found out about YOUmedia through her friends. She attends school nearby and is a veteran who has been visiting YOUmedia for about two years. She usually comes several times a month and stays for less than an hour. Kayla has worked on several school projects at YOUmedia and is often found checking out and returning books. Kayla also talks with friends and staff and checks her email and Facebook accounts. She has never attended a workshop at YOUmedia and says she is not a "tech creator" or a "workshop-er." She writes poetry in her free time but prefers not to share it with other people. She is also very involved in theater outside of YOUmedia. If there were a workshop at YOUmedia related to acting or theater-tech, she says that she would happily participate.

Relationship with Staff: Even though Kayla has not collaborated with a mentor on a project, she still feels close to one mentor in the space with whom she enjoys discussing their shared interest of biking. She also enjoys talking with staff members. "I talk about books. It's fun. I get some suggestions."

Benefits of YOUmedia: Despite her lack of participation, Kayla still reports that she has gained knowledge through her close relationships with the adults at YOUmedia. She says that because of her time in the space and the social interactions she has had, she has learned to be more open and confident in talking to new people. She feels more optimistic about the world because there are adults who respect teens at YOUmedia, and she hopes that adult respect for teens can spread throughout the rest of the world.

Floaters

Floaters visit YOUmedia to play video games, use the computers, hang out with friends, and attend open mic; they are likely to do many of these things on a single visit. When on a computer, Floaters are playing games, watching a movie or YouTube, checking Facebook or email, surfing the web, and/or doing their homework. Nearly two-thirds of Floaters have visited for more than a year, and two-thirds have visited at least weekly. Almost 80 percent of the Floaters are male, and one-third attend a selective enrollment high school. Over half the Floaters gained a new interest at YOUmedia and participate in YOUmedia's formal offerings. Forty-one percent attended at least two types of workshops and an additional 15 percent attended one type of workshop.

DANIELA: A YOUmedia "Floater"

Participation at YOUmedia: Daniela learned about YOUmedia from her friends, and she has been coming to the space for over 1.5 years. She is a regular visitor who comes to YOUmedia three or four times per week and considers it her "afterschool hangout spot." Daniela comes directly from school and stays for two to three hours. She has expanded her participation at YOUmedia in the time that she has been coming to the space. At first, she only hung out with friends and played video games. Now, she also messes around on the computer and works on projects. Although she still spends much of her time with her friends and playing video games, she has also attended workshops on a variety of topics with a particular interest in art, including graphic design, music production, photography, gaming, and writing. She attended several of these workshops multiple times, but she dropped out due to time constraints and other commitments.

Relationship with Staff: Daniela works with a staff member on a project about once per month. She feels a strong personal connection with the adult staff, stating that she can relate to them better than to other adults in her life. Although she has had trusting relationships with teachers, she feels that her relationship with the YOUmedia adults is different because they care about her as a person, not just as a student. From the staff she has learned "to keep your cool. To keep calm...You have to keep your calm if you plan on moving on."

Benefits of YOUmedia: Although she has not been heavily involved with digital media production, she reports that she has improved at posting items like stories online and creating and using multiple types of media. She says she now feels comfortable helping other teens use the equipment in the space. She also feels that she has learned some social skills in the space. Learning how to interact with boys is particularly valuable for Daniela because she goes to an all-girl school.

Experimenters

Experimenters visit YOUmedia to use the equipment and to work on an interest—mostly music. Instead of using the music studio, they take advantage of the computers and keyboards to practice and write music. They often chat or work with friends, but they rarely interact with the adults. Almost two-thirds of the Experimenters have visited for a year or less and three-fourths have visited at least weekly. Three-fourths of the Experimenters are male, and only 13 percent attend a selective enrollment high school. Even though many Experimenters are newcomers to YOUmedia, three-quarters said they have

28

been introduced to a new interest, and over half have attended at least two types of workshops and an additional 21 percent attended one type.

CARTER: A YOUmedia Experimenter

Participation at YOUmedia: Carter learned about YOUmedia from a relative and from his friends. He is a newcomer, visiting YOUmedia once or twice a week for less than a year. Carter primarily uses the space as an afterschool hangout and homework spot. However, he also spends a lot of time on the music equipment, experimenting with beats and remixing songs. Although he has been in the music studio before, he almost exclusively uses the freestanding music equipment in the space. In addition to his musical interests, Carter is developing an interest in photography. He has attended at least one photography workshop. Carter explores and experiments with music making, but he does not often produce finished products at YOUmedia.

Relationship with Staff: Carter does not feel a personal connection with the staff at YOUmedia, but still says that he relates to them better than to other adults and that he trusts them. He says the staff listens to teens better than adult family members or teachers. He does not feel that they necessarily share his interests, although he says that he has made friends with similar interests.

Benefits of YOUmedia: Carter feels that his experience at YOUmedia has given him a better understanding of his opportunities after high school. He specifically feels more knowledgeable about pursuing further studies and a career in photography or in music. Carter also feels that he learned "how to socialize with different people. I was shy when I first came here." This helped him take advantage of opportunities for collaboration with other teens that he would not otherwise have had outside of YOUmedia.

Creators

Creators are the teens who are the most heavily involved with YOUmedia and its offerings and who work on their interests there. These include creating music in the studio, working on art and graphic design projects, creating podcasts, blogging, and writing and performing poetry. We found two main subgroups among the Creators: music Creators and other Creators.

Music Creators are found in the recording studio producing music. About half of music Creators have visited for more than a year, all of them visit at least weekly, and most (82 percent) stay for least two hours when they visit. The vast majority (86 percent) of music Creators are male, two-thirds are African American male, and only 14 percent attend a selective enrollment

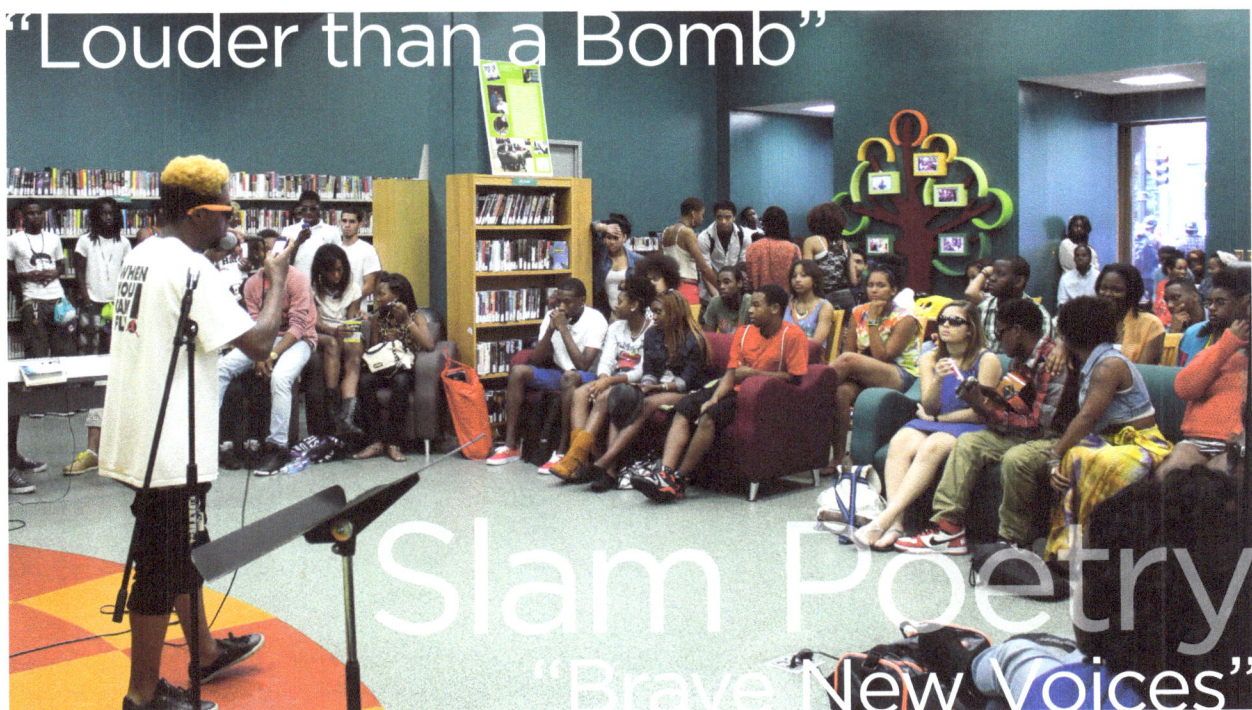

high school. Music Creators are active participants in YOUmedia. Almost all report being introduced to a new interest, 84 percent have attended at least one workshop, and 40 percent have worked with an adult at least monthly.

Other Creators are found throughout the space working on their particular interests. Two-thirds have visited for more than a year and three-fourths visit at least weekly. Half of other Creators are female, and half attend a selective enrollment high school. Other Creators also are active participants in YOUmedia. Almost all have gained a new interest, three-fourths have attended at least one workshop, and 70 percent have worked with an adult at least monthly.

ARIANNA: A YOUmedia Music Creator

Participation at YOUmedia: Arianna discovered YOUmedia through a summer program that visited YOUmedia to use the equipment. When she learned about YOUmedia's music studio, she was thrilled about the opportunities it would provide her and was especially excited about the possibilities of working with adults and peers who could teach her new things. Arianna has been visiting YOUmedia for over two years. She visits at least twice a week and usually stays for one or two hours. When Arianna first visited YOUmedia, she mostly hung out with her friends and messed around on the computer. Although she continues to engage in these activities, she now also works on her music, including singing, writing, and producing. She participates in music production workshops and is often in the music studio. She does not use the YOUmedia social network because she does not find it useful.

Arianna participated in the record label workshop and has worked on the What's Going On...Now, Ladies of the Media, and Steppenwolf Theatre projects. She collaborated closely with both a friend and a staff member on the What's Going On...Now project, for which she wrote and performed music.

Relationship with Staff: Arianna is friendly with all of the adults and chats with most of them about either workshops or general topics. She has a close relationship with one adult, with whom she collaborates on music projects and in whom she confides personal matters. She says that this staff member introduces

her to knowledge and teaches her things about music production that exceed her expectations. She also says that their relationship increases her self-confidence.

Benefits of YOUmedia: When Arianna first visited YOUmedia, she could sing but had no digital productions skills. She now knows how to use GarageBand and considers herself a music producer, which, she says, makes her stand above her peers. She reports that the honest feedback on her music that she receives at YOUmedia helps her express her ideas and be more open to feedback, as well as improves the quality of her work. Arianna believes strongly that her involvement with YOUmedia opens up opportunities to her that she would not have otherwise. "I have access to things that I couldn't have used before to get what I need to get done. And now I feel like what was already within me has been exposed to me or revealed to me, and now I'm using it."

HADDON: A YOUmedia Non-Music Creator

Participation at YOUmedia: Haddon first learned about YOUmedia from his friends at school when they told him that the library has the video game Rock Band available. This piqued Haddon's interest, so he visited the space and has been coming back consistently for over 1.5 years. On average, he visits the space more than three times per week and stays for one to two hours each visit. Haddon reports that he spends most of his time at YOUmedia playing video games, messing around on the computer, and hanging out with his friends. But he is also heavily involved in two workshops: graphic design and gaming. Through these workshops and on his own, Haddon consistently produces written blogs, audio podcasts, videos, and graphic design materials. In these formal and informal activities, Haddon frequently learns from and works closely with adults and collaborates with other teens. He often posts his work on various websites (e.g., Facebook, Tumblr, YouTube, and Twitter) due to his desire to become "internet famous." He posts less frequently on YOUmedia Online because he believes that audience is limited.

Relationship with Staff: Haddon feels strong personal connections with several of the adults at YOUmedia. He trusts them and thinks they are

really cool and friendly. He feels like he can talk to them about anything. He describes them as "nerds." He says he has learned from staff that there are nice adults in the world. He is excited that there are adults who have his same interests and that it is possible to turn those interests into a career. "Oh, man. YOUmedia just like made my life like a million times better just because I meet adults who I wish I could be when I grow up. When I grow up, I want to become a YOUmedia mentor."

Benefits of YOUmedia: Prior to coming to YOUmedia, Haddon was actively pursuing his interests in video games and computers on his own, mostly using the internet to learn new skills. However, through his participation in formal and informal activities in the space, Haddon learns a variety of digital media skills. Through the graphic design workshop, Haddon learned how to use Photoshop software to create and edit images and how to use electronic tablets to create graphic design projects. The video game workshop provided Haddon with technical skills for creating a podcast. Developing a new, more critical way to discuss video games has improved his writing skills and helped him with presenting information to an audience. He states that YOUmedia increases his interest in technology by providing a space to connect with others who have the same interests. He also feels that YOUmedia increases his confidence in technology and makes him more confident in himself overall.

"I have access to things that I couldn't have used before to get what I need to get done. And now I feel like what was already within me has been exposed to me or revealed to me, and now I'm using it."

In addition to the physical space, YOUmedia has an online space that is a social networking site built on the iRemix Social Learning Platform originally developed by DYN and currently managed by Remix Learning. The YOUmedia social network is a closed network (teens must register to participate) that is accessible 24 hours a day and that provides teens with opportunities to interact with peers and mentors when the library is closed or otherwise inaccessible. While it was originally designed to give teens a place to interact outside of the physical space and to support their learning by providing feedback loops and extending workshops, the staff is now emphasizing the importance of the site as an aid to learning. Teens and staff participate in the YOUmedia social network. Teens create personal pages, join online groups, post and comment on multimedia items, and send messages to their peers; staff members post their own work and critique the work of teens.

Teen Participation in the YOUmedia Social Network

Survey results show that most teens do not use the site to socialize with their peers. Two-thirds of teens reported never having used the YOUmedia social network (see Figure 8). Most of them (55 percent) said they did not know about it; others said they found it difficult to use, had little incentive to use it, or preferred other social networking sites.

FIGURE 8

Few teens use the YOUmedia social network

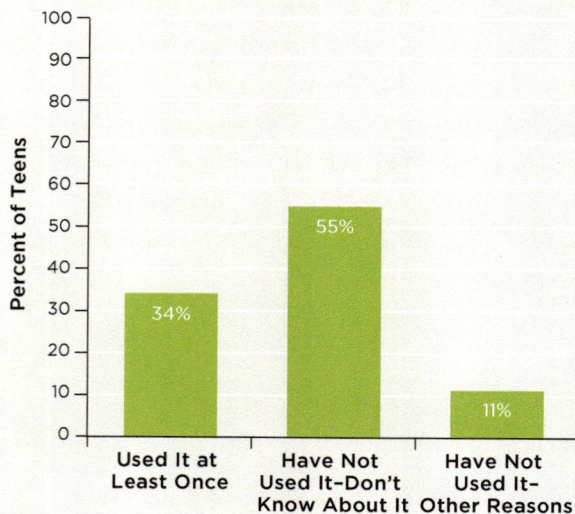

Source: 2012 YOUmedia Survey

In interviews, many teens said they preferred Facebook and other larger social networks because of existing connections with their friends and family. As one teen said about the YOUmedia social network, "I have no friends on there yet." Another described its niche as one that may not draw teens:

> And I feel like the...YOUmedia social networking site is a very small number of people. Because some of my Facebook friends or many of my Facebook friends either don't come to YOUmedia or don't even live in town. Or in the country, really...plus, they're not always necessarily my age. Whereas I feel like YOUmedia's social networking site is specifically for the urban, adolescent artist. And because that's a very small demographic...if the appeal of a social networking site is the number of people that you know on it, Facebook has the larger pull.

For teens who are not heavily involved in workshops or digital media production, the YOUmedia social network lacks appeal. As one teen said, "I feel like that's something where people would use to, like, publish their work and stuff, and I'm really not that kind of person."

After the surveys and interviews, Remix Learning worked to address some of the concerns raised by youth. They modified the site to allow teens to push their postings to some of the public sites, including Facebook, Twitter, and Tumblr.[30]

The YOUmedia Social Network Supports Learning Activities

The YOUmedia social network has improved the learning process for some teens by providing them with opportunities to get feedback on their projects. In interviews, many staff members mentioned a core group of "regulars" who make up most of its users. These teens, who participate in workshops and produce media, use it to get feedback on their projects from staff and peers. As one staff member stated, "for a lot of them it's feedback. So posting what they're working on to make sure they're on track, improving and getting that feedback from mentors but also getting feedback from other students."

The staff members who have been most successful in getting teens to use the YOUmedia social network have made clear connections between it and their workshops. The Word Slam Poetry Team has been especially successful at this by encouraging teens to share their work, to provide feedback to each other, and to receive critiques from knowledgeable adults. They note that the social network meets a distinct need in the online worlds of these teens:

So Facebook for a lot of them is, 'Alright, this is where I just kick it and talk to my friends. I might just put up anything randomly. Twitter, these are just my random thoughts. YOUmedia, this is the place where I'm going to get critiqued, feedback, and connect with students who are creative.' So I think for them it's seeing these clear pathways in terms of what each space that they use is for.

The YOUmedia social network online space provides some teens with a place to share their work with a wider audience. One mentor described teens who "really have a desire to show their work artistically. They are really excited about it, they want to show it off, and they want to talk a little bit about it on the online space."

YOUmedia Online Joins Hive Chicago
Midway through the study, two major events affected the YOUmedia social network. First, YOUmedia joined Hive Chicago, a set of organizations dedicated to providing youth opportunities to pursue varied interests both online and in physical spaces. This led to opening up the social network to youth from many other organizations that make up the Chicago Hive Learning Network (HLN)[31] in order to encourage collaboration between and integration of these organizations. It also meant rebranding the site and changing its management. The aesthetics of the YOUmedia social network were changed from YOUmedia's logo and colors to those of the HLN, and the URL was modified to be more reflective of the HLN.

The second event that occurred at about the same time was that Remix Learning updated the underlying iRemix platform. This resulted in a number of usability problems.[32] Some parts of Hive Chicago were cumbersome for teens to use and may have discouraged participation in YOUmedia's social network. The URL of Hive Chicago is difficult for teens to remember, registering can be time consuming, and it is hard to remember log-in information. In our interviews, both adults and teens mentioned that the YOUmedia social network had become more difficult to use and was much less user-friendly than other social networking sites. As one individual explained:

For instance, if you log into Facebook and you want to post a picture, you hit two buttons. You know, you click twice. And I think if there's really more than one or two clicks, people are really turned off, right. With our site it's like step, upon step, upon step—like click, click, click, click, click. It's frustrating. It takes a long time. The site freezes. There's just...a lot of technical errors that happen.

The lack of continuity between YOUmedia Online and Hive Chicago, combined with the updating of the iRemix platform, caused the YOUmedia social network to lose many of its regular users. Since then, the leadership at Remix Learning has changed, and they are working to rectify these difficulties. They have improved the overall infrastructure of Hive Chicago and its usability, and they have introduced new features to make it easier and more desirable for engaged youth to use the site.[33]

33

CHAPTER 3
Benefits of YOUmedia

In the last chapter, we saw that YOUmedia's teens participate in its offerings in a variety of ways. In this chapter, we share teens' perceptions of the benefits they receive from participating in YOUmedia. Specifically we address these questions:

Does YOUmedia offer a safe, welcoming place where teens have opportunities to pursue their interests? What benefits do teens perceive from their participation in YOUmedia? New and or expanded interests? New skills in digital media? Greater expertise in an area of interest? Expanded use of library resources? Skills that benefit schoolwork? Greater understanding of future college and career choices?

There is broad agreement among the teens that YOUmedia provides them with a safe and welcoming place. They recognize that YOUmedia is a place expressly for them, where they feel accepted regardless of who they are. Teens know that YOUmedia is a place where they can pursue their interests and that they have friends and mentors at YOUmedia who have similar interests. Among all types of participants, the portion of teens who work on an interest at YOUmedia is growing over time. Many teens report benefiting from YOUmedia, including improving digital media skills; strengthening academic skills; and/or gaining a better understanding of opportunities after high school.

YOUmedia Provides Teens with a Safe and Welcoming Place

Among the developers' aspirations was for YOUmedia to be a safe place where youth could meet, socialize, and build a community together. The design of YOUmedia also encompassed adults who would develop strong relationships with teens, teach them new skills, and mentor them as they pursued their intersts. For the most part, YOUmedia fulfilled these early aspirations,

regardless of the ways in which the teens participate in YOUmedia. In response to a 2012 survey question, two-thirds of YOUmedia's teens indicated they feel they are an important member of the YOUmedia community (those who disagreed did not attend regularly). Based on the 2011 survey, over half (54 percent) of the teens described the safe and welcoming nature of YOUmedia as a reason they visit. Teens said they come to YOUmedia because it is a place where they are physically or emotionally safe, feel a sense of belonging, and/or have fun. The following are representative of responses to open-ended items from the 2011 survey and comments from interviews with case-study teens:

Some youth described the physical and emotional safety:

- I visit YOUmedia because it is a safe place to come hang out with friends.

- This is one of my safe places. I'm not in a dangerous situation.

- I feel safe. There's not a lotta fights. You know, for a lotta strangers in one room, having a lot of movement and they don't really get in a fight.

- Because I feel like this is one of the few places I won't be judged or criticized for my thought process. It's a genuine space.

- I feel a good vibe in this library every time I come in here. People don't have attitudes and stuff.

- It's real chill, and everybody's nice and open.

Others expressed a sense of belonging:

- It is a great place to be. Definitely have built a family with everyone here. I can't imagine being anywhere else if YOUmedia didn't exist.

- Because my friends come here, and I've seen it grow into something really cool. I think it's a great place for kids who need a space away from home.

- Because I find it cool that a place has been created for teens that is positive socializing and intellectual projects.

- Because there are teens here my age I can bond with and it has a very comfortable environment.

- YOUmedia is an amazing place to connect with others and listen to and learn about other people.

Young people enjoy being at YOUmedia:

- Because it's super, awesome, fun, positive, and safe.

- To hang with friends and have fun.

YOUmedia Supports Teens' Interests

To the designers of YOUmedia, teen interests were paramount. Our year one report described how the staff made teens' interests central to the activities at YOUmedia, and this remains just as important today. The teens clearly perceive this; the vast majority feel that YOUmedia supports their interests. Eighty-nine percent think that at YOUmedia it is cool to be excited about your interests. Not only is it cool to be excited about your interests, but almost all report that they have friends and mentors with whom they share interests **(see Figure 9)**. Recall that the youth viewed all adults as mentors, whether they were CPL or DYN staff members.

YOUmedia's support of teen interests is further substantiated by comparing the portion who reported working on an interest when they first came to YOUmedia to the portion who reported working on an interest in spring 2012. In **Figure 10**, notice the differences between the blue and green bars. Green bars represent the teens who were working on an interest when they first visited YOUmedia; the blue bars show that by spring 2012 (when they completed the survey), a larger portion of teens were pursuing an interest (e.g., producing music, video, or graphic designs; or gaming). Regardless of the participation category, over time each group increased the proportion who were working on an interest. In the percent of teens involved with an interest, Experimenters and Creators showed the biggest growth and Floaters and Socializers showed the smallest growth.

Students at All Levels of Participation Reported Improvement in Digital Media Skills, Especially the Creators

About half (57 percent) of all teens report improving in one or more digital media skills because of YOUmedia. The creators were the most likely to show improvement, with 84 percent reporting improved skills in one or more areas and 60 percent reporting improved skills in two to six areas **(see Figure 11)**.

As expected, based on their interests and activities, the Creators improved their skills in recording

FIGURE 9

YOUmedia support of teen interest

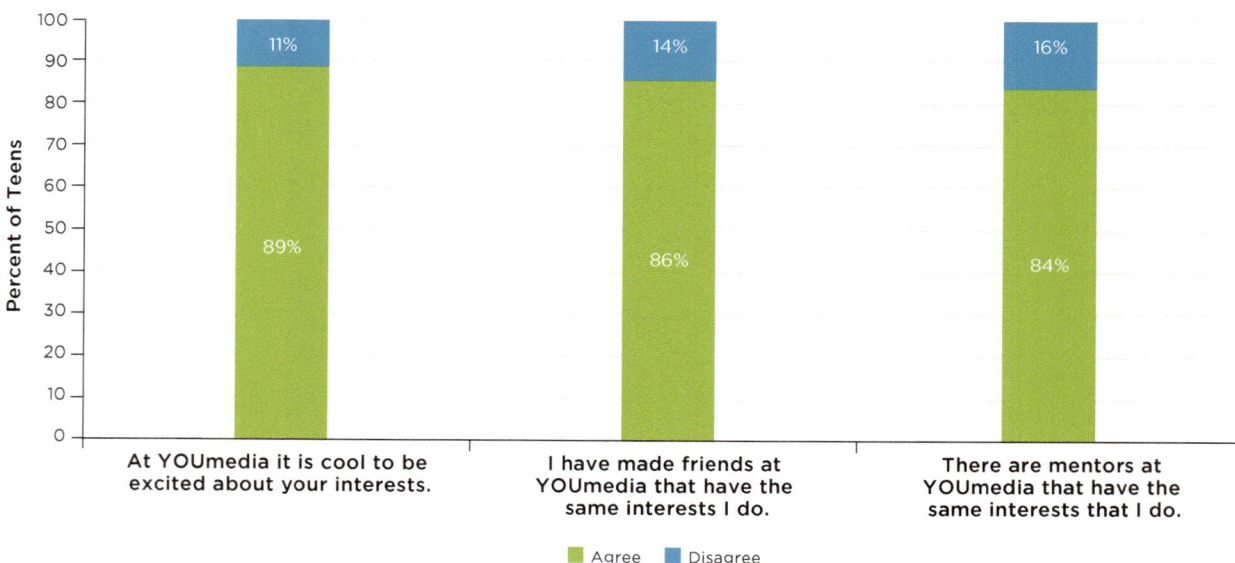

Source: 2012 YOUmedia Survey
Note: Teens viewed all adults as mentors

FIGURE 10

Teens' inclination to work on their interests grows over time

Percent working on an interest when they first came to YOUmedia compared to now (spring 2012)

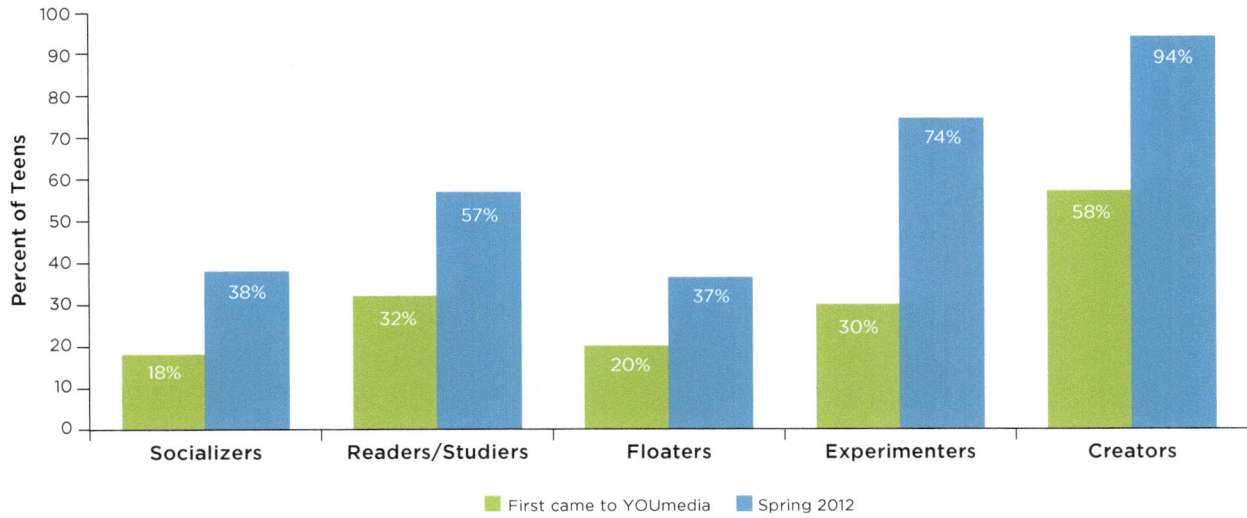

Source: 2012 YOUmedia Survey

FIGURE 11

A majority of the creators and about half of others improved their digital media skills due to YOUmedia

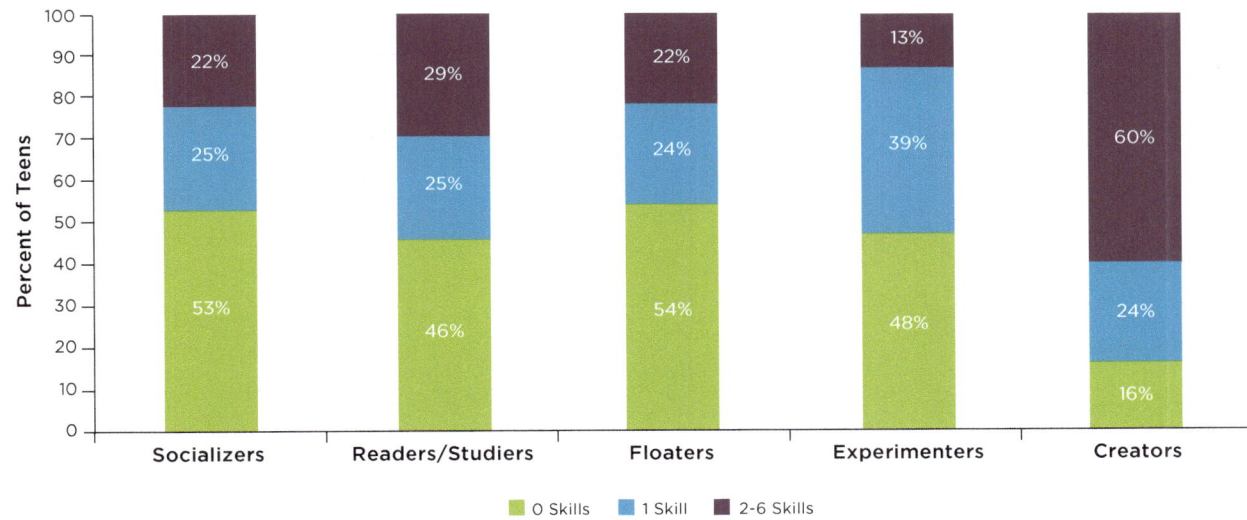

Source: 2012 YOUmedia Survey

TABLE 2

YOUmedia teens improved in a variety of areas

Percent Reporting Improvement by Type					
	Socializers	Readers/ Studiers	Floaters	Experimenters	Creators
Making a Graphic Design	0	20	17	4	20
Making a Video	25	27	20	22	40
Using Multiple Types of Media to Create	10	16	7	9	33
Posting Something on the Internet	28	14	13	34	27
Producing a Podcast	0	0	4	0	9
Creating a Website	0	9	7	4	13
Recording Music	18	9	9	35	56
Making an Animation	0	14	11	4	11

Spring 2012 Youth Survey

Note: Teens could check more than one.

music, making videos, using multiple types of media to create something, and posting something on the internet (**see Table 2**). Because the preponderance of the Experimenters pursue music at YOUmedia, it is not surprising that their most commonly improved skill is recording music. Among the other groups, almost one-quarter improved in making videos and small proportions improved in a variety of areas.

Students at All Participation Levels Reported Improvement in Academic Skills, Including Schoolwork, Writing Skills, and Communication with Adults

Overall, a majority of teens reported that YOUmedia has helped them with their academic skills. Over half reported that YOUmedia has helped them with their schoolwork, improved their writing skills, and improved their communication with adults. This varies across types of participation, with the Creators reporting the most favorably in all areas (**see Figure 12**).

A large majority of the Creators indicated that what they learned at YOUmedia spilled over into their academic lives and helped them with schoolwork, writing skills, and communication with adults. Even the Socializers, who spend the least time on digital and other projects, felt they gained from YOUmedia. It appears that enough of them participated in work-

shops, interacted with the staff, and understood the importance of developing and pursuing interests that they strengthened their academic skills. The culture that almost uniformly says it is cool to pursue one's interests also may have had benefits. All of this suggests that advantages may accrue even for teens who are using the space in more recreational ways.

One of the specific research questions was whether participation in YOUmedia expanded teens' use of library resources. While we do not have much evidence on this question, we know that for one-quarter of the YOUmedia youth, the Readers/Studiers, consulting the library staff and using books and computers were main activities. In addition, **Figure 12** shows that they believed their participation in YOUmedia yielded important benefits. About two-thirds agreed with the statement that YOUmedia helped them improve schoolwork and communication with adults, and almost half said it helped improve writing. Thus, the books and the library staff were particularly important for this group. We know also that a sprinkling of teens associated with the other types also reported use of the library resources.

Interviews with 11 of the 23 case-study teens provide examples of how participation at YOUmedia connects to what teens do at school:

Schoolwork: Six teens mentioned that YOUmedia supports them in their schoolwork. Two of them commented that their schoolwork had improved simply

FIGURE 12

Youmedia helped teens improve academic skills

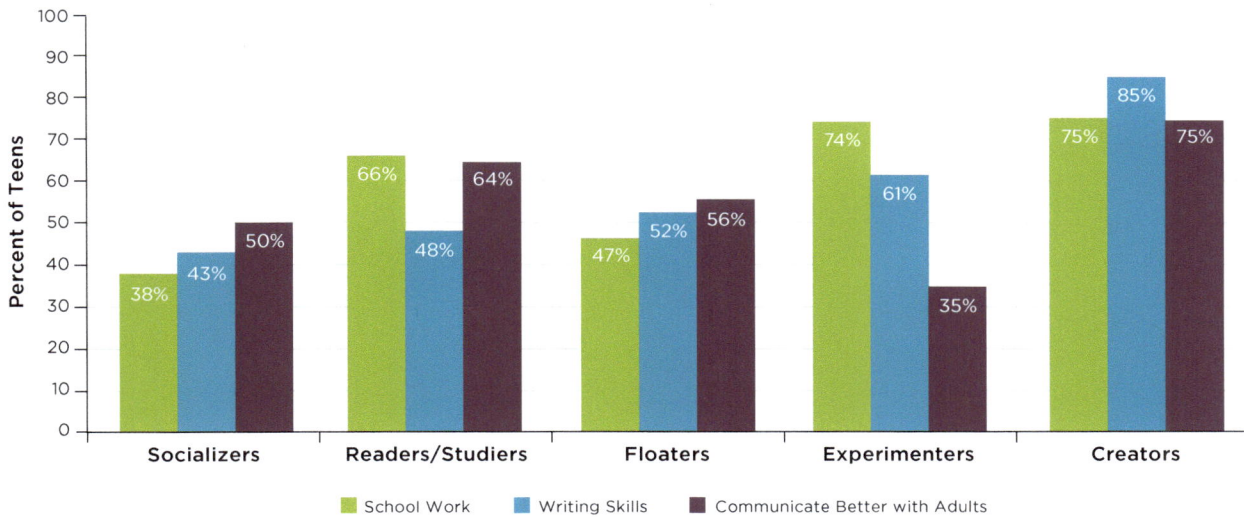

Source: 2012 YOUmedia Survey

because they had learned about computers and how to use them correctly. For three others, it was using the resources that YOUmedia provides to help them complete their schoolwork. These included reference materials, word processing programs, and other software that was not available on their home computers. One teen added that YOUmedia makes him more effective in studying, doing his homework, and interacting with teachers. He went on to say that "it fosters intellectual creativity, which really works well in school because you're very creative and you're more into what you're learning."

Writing Skills: Three teens mentioned that the reading and writing they do at YOUmedia are helpful for school. One teen said that working on the YOUlit magazine exposed her to new kinds of poetry and literature and gave her experience editing text. Another teen mentioned that working on a project based on the book *Neverwhere* provided helpful experience with reading and writing. One teen mentioned that the writing workshops she attended at YOUmedia helped her with writing for school.

Communication Skills: Two teens mentioned that YOUmedia helped them improve their communication skills. One said that through YOUmedia he has learned to approach people better, and the other said that YOUmedia has made him better at presenting to other people.

Students at All Levels of Participation Reported Increased Awareness of Post-High School Opportunities

Overall, almost three-fourths of teens reported that YOUmedia has helped them understand more about the opportunities available to them after high school. While the Creators and Experimenters were the most likely to report being helped, almost two-thirds of the other teens also indicated this benefit (**see Figure 13**).

In interviews, the case-study teens indicated that YOUmedia benefits them in several ways. First, it provides them with resources like college and scholarship reference books that help them navigate the selection and application process. In addition, staff members provide individual teens with guidance and encouragement about their future plans regarding college and careers. Finally, YOUmedia's workshops and projects expose them to and foster interests in a variety of fields that are illustrative of possible areas of study or careers. These include art, journalism, video editing, music, film, writing, and literature.

FIGURE 13

YOUmedia helped teens understand opportunities after high school

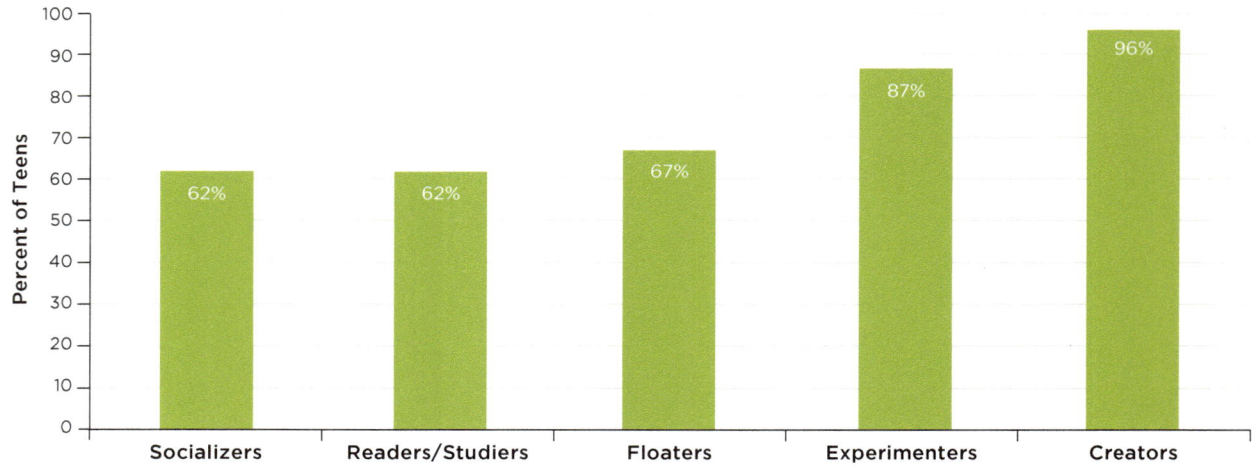

Source: 2012 YOUmedia Survey

40

CHAPTER 4

Adult Support, Teen Choice, and Program Challenges

In the last chapter, we saw that teens benefited in a variety of ways from their participation in YOUmedia. We know that the adults were an instrumental part of their experiences, and this chapter further explores the ways these adults get acquainted with the youth, support their engagement, and provide broader advice and guidance.

WE ADDRESS THE FOLLOWING QUESTIONS:

How is the program designed to engage youth in pursuing their interests? (This chapter builds further on the discussion in Chapter 1.)

What role does staff play in introducing teens to resources, sparking their interests, and developing their skills?

Recall from Chapter 1 that the hybrid design of YOUmedia allows teens a great deal of latitude. The design grew out of the partnering organizations, each with its own distinct mission and culture. Embedded in the partnership were elements of both unstructured and structured activities.[34] Staff members play a range of supporting roles, and they design learning activities to respond to the myriad needs of the teens. We describe their roles here, and we outline organizational challenges in meeting teens' needs.

Staff Members Work to Bridge Social and Learning Worlds by Developing Genuine Personal Connections

The fact that YOUmedia's design merges teens' social and learning worlds requires adults to bridge the two as they support teens in developing existing interests and finding new ones. However, this is not an easy task. Not only do the staff need to play various roles beyond teaching content to teens but they also must carefully balance engaging teens while simultaneously

providing them with learning opportunities to support their skill development. A crucial part of achieving this balance is initiating and nurturing personal and genuine connections with teens. Because teens do not always visit YOUmedia regularly, relationship building is an incremental process. Only when every chance to connect with teens is maximized can adults in their role as mentors begin to link teens with appropriate learning opportunities. A staff member at YOUmedia, offers, "I will engage them for a long time before I even start talking to them about workshops...you need to get to know teens." Another states,

The teens feel like we've taken the time to learn their names and learn what they're interested in and kind of make a connection with them, even if they're just checking out a laptop...I don't think we would have as many kids returning if it was an impersonal interaction. So that is why it's important to have friendly people working [here] and helping out kids.

In addition to being friendly and making teens feel welcome in the space, staff members have to be able to relate to teens on matters of importance to them. As one of them explains, "They see us as very culturally engaged and culturally relevant. I think they not only see us as people who can talk to them as adults but also on their level..."

Gauging teens' interests and skills. At YOUmedia, relationships permit informal assessment of teens' interests, allowing adults to connect teens with resources that can best support those interests within the space. YOUmedia has no process to systematically assess teens' interests, so staff members utilize their relationships with teens to gauge their interests, their proficiency with digital media tools, and their ability to create products. One mentor describes how getting

41

to know teens and encouraging them to participate in structured learning activities go hand-in-hand:

You have the workshop, which you want to get [teens] into, and the only way you can get those [teens] is to ask them, 'What do you do?' I think the more trustworthy or comfortable you get in the relationship with the teen, it's easier to sort of bring them into projects. It's like a dance, but at the end of the day, I just hope that they get involved with something at least once while they're here.

Social and emotional needs. Beyond supporting their interests, adults' interactions with teens must address teens' various social and emotional needs. Adults discover these social and emotional needs while maintaining an ongoing relationship with teens, and, as a result, their roles often extend beyond teaching or sharing their expertise as artists and library professionals. As part of their professional development, for example, YOUmedia staff advocated obtaining training from a social worker for adolescents. The training covered concrete strategies for helping teens access case management and mental health resources, as well as mandated reporting procedures for instances in which teens disclose to the staff risk of physical harm to themselves.

Clearly, as adults mentor teens, their responsibilities run the gamut, from helping teens with homework and other academic projects, to providing teens with resources inside and outside of YOUmedia, to augmenting their digital media interests, to offering social and emotional support to individuals.

A staff member's description of her role reflects this versatility:

I think of myself as someone who provides students with information resources. That can be books; that can be websites; that can be random factoids and tidbits. It can be a whole host of things. Because I do a workshop, I'm also teaching them digital skills. And then also I'm just someone they can talk to about whatever they need to talk to me about. It doesn't have to be something related to digital media. It could just be something really random or big in their life that's serious.

Other studies have found that adults' ability to play multiple roles is a salient feature for engaging teens. One study showed that youth valued the mentoring aspect of their relationships with adults, which involved helping them stay on track in their academics and motivating them to participate in activities as well as the "confidant" aspects of the relationship. Youth also appreciated discussing their personal problems and expressing their feelings to adults they did not view as "having power over them" in the same way as teachers at school.[35]

Teens appreciate and value the mentors. Teens' reactions to or comments about the adults, whom they viewed as mentors, suggest that the staff members have succeeded in building positive relationships with them. **Figure 14** shows that a large majority of the teens feel that they have a personal connection with a mentor, and almost all of the teens trust the mentors. This is notable in view of the large number of teens (350 to 500) who may visit YOUmedia each week. This is also crucial because prior research on out-of-school programs involving digital media indicates that human relationships, such as mentoring connections between adults and youth, are fundamental to the success of the organization—more so than the technological tools.[36]

FIGURE 14

Teens are connected to the mentors

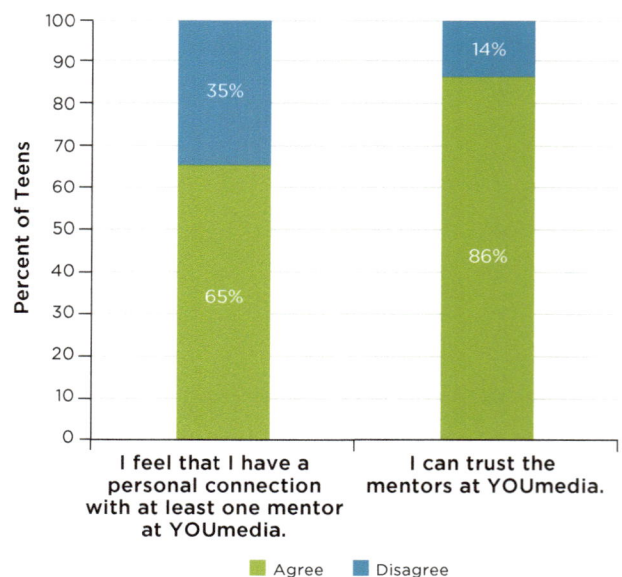

Source: 2012 YOUmedia Survey

In our interviews, YOUmedia teens illustrated the multiple ways in which staff members support their varied interests—interests that were specific to each individual teen. Some of what we heard is highlighted:

- They have book discussions about...interesting books. And me and Claudia share some really good... recipes. (**YOUmedia SOCIALIZER**)

- They give me a computer to watch anime, books to read on anime and they give me the words to put inspiration for poetry. (**YOUmedia FLOATER**)

- ...People in here are into [writing] a lot. People...have extensive knowledge...they're all college-educated professionals. They can help you with it...intellectually, technologically, and all that. It's the environment and the mentors that foster creativity and...it reinforces your interests. It makes you feel good about yourself... (**YOUmedia CREATOR**)

- Mentors support teens by doing the podcasts, by doing all these little groups, by supplying you with any kind of help that you possibly need or want. They always have your back, and I really love that. And, they will cheer you up when you're down. (**YOUmedia FLOATER**)

- They have the workshops. And like Jeffrey, you can show him some of your artwork and he can give you tips on how to do things better for your next piece. And when it comes to Evaluna and writing the songs, she really helps you think about what comes next, you know. (**YOUmedia READER/STUDIER**)

To more fully understand the creative process in which teens and adults engage, see **sidebar** *The Final Cut: A View into a Podcast Production Process*, **p. 44.** It describes the steps involved in producing a film review and illustrates the importance of close collaboration between teens and staff and the staff's responsiveness to teens' interests.

Teen choice: A challenge for adults in helping teens build skills. Recall that a large portion of teens are not involved in workshops, podcasts, music recordings, YOUlit, or other structured activities. The balance between respecting teens' freedom to socialize while engaging them in formal learning activities proves to be challenging. One staff member's quote about this balancing act is representative of what we heard from other adults at YOUmedia:

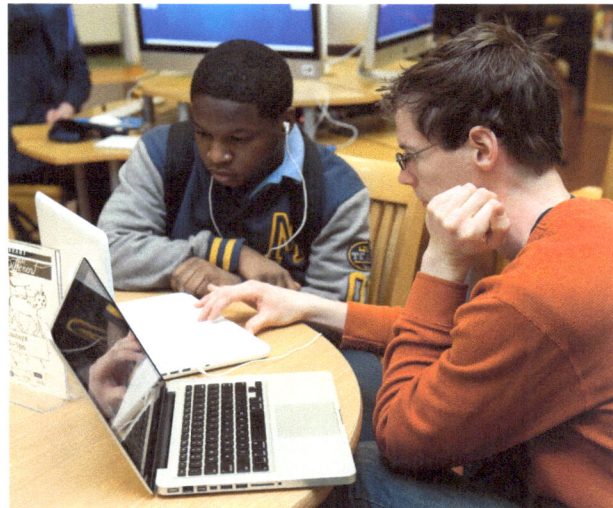

I feel like [for] a group of kids, this is just a space where the beginning and the end of it for them is hanging out, which is fine. As a staff, we try and push kids. We don't want to be willing to let kids come into the space and let stuff go for granted.

Fundamentally, staff members have to accept that some teens come to YOUmedia only to socialize because the space sanctions this type of engagement. For many staff members, and for program leadership and potential funders, this provides a key challenge: how to attain the ultimate goal of promoting learning opportunities and resources without being too proscriptive of teen freedom.

The Design of Formal Learning Activities Changed over Time to Better Support Teen Learning and Engagement

Because YOUmedia has goals around improving teens' skills and exposing them to new interests, adults spend much of their time figuring out how to best structure formal learning opportunities. The hybrid design holds implications for the way formal learning activities are structured within the space. Formal learning activities at YOUmedia originally were designed as multisession workshops with learning objectives intended to sequentially build skills, which is similar to the way most classes function in a school. However, as described below, the variability and unpredictability of teen

The Final Cut: A View into a Podcast Production Process

Micah has been heavily involved in creative production for the majority of the 2.5 years he has been coming to YOUmedia. He is a contributor to the Video Game Blog, a collaborative podcast produced by several teens and a staff member who analyzes and critiques video games. While the Video Game Blog offers a fun collaboration with friends, Micah's favorite project is the Final Cut podcast—a production he created with a mentor.

When he first started coming to YOUmedia, Micah says his creative opportunities were provided to him through creating the Video Game Blog to channel the interests and skills of a group of teens interested in video games. Although Micah enjoys video games and the collaborative podcast, his true interest lies in film. Skylar, the staff member who oversees the Video Game Blog, also has an academic background and personal interest in film. Micah was able to create the Final Cut podcast with her, which provides the creative control and ownership of the podcast that is his goal.

> Video Game Blog was a project created for me. I did it. And our workshop—our critiquing—that was created for me. Then I started creating things for myself to do. I created the Final Cut podcast. I created some things for me to do. Those opportunities still exist, but I've done more of the creating part than I originally did. —Micah

Micah says he and Skylar generally start preparing for a podcast about two weeks in advance of recording. After choosing the movie they are going to review, they make sure they have plenty of time to watch and discuss it. They also communicate about it on Twitter. Then they schedule time in the recording studio and set up the recording equipment they need. The recording of the podcast takes about an 1.5 hours. Micah says the operation is very efficient and requires little editing...just the addition of music at the beginning and end. He and Skylar continue to collaborate after each podcast through discussions of ways to improve and potential future topics.

Recently, he and Skylar reviewed the film *The Social Network*. Micah felt that it was an all-around good film, with good acting, writing, and production. He said that he and Skylar only had one minor disagreement when they reviewed one scene, which was a minor disagreement. Micah says this is very unusual because they usually disagree more when they analyze a film. He feels that their debates add to the quality of their discussions because they represent different points of view and make the podcast more entertaining. Micah occasionally shares his podcasts with his father and brother, who he says enjoy listening to his critiques. The podcast is available through a website dedicated to the podcast, which is connected to SoundCloud, an audio distribution website. Micah says the Final Cut generally receives around 20 to 30 plays, which is even more than the Video Game Blog usually gets.

In the process of creating and operating the Final Cut, Micah says that he has learned to better analyze movies and formulate his own arguments. He also says that he has learned to communicate and collaborate one-on-one, rather than in a bigger group as he does with the Video Game Blog. In terms of technical skills, he has learned how to better utilize GarageBand, a sound recording and editing program. Micah feels that these skills will help him if he chooses to pursue a career as a film critic, or any career that involves podcasting, which he feels is a growing subset of the film community. He also believes that his communication skills and ability to formulate and execute ideas will be useful regardless of his future career choice.

> I've learned how to read movies more... [it's] made me more inclined to develop my own arguments instead of regurgitating that of film critics. —Micah

attendance and engagement led staff to develop and implement new types of learning activities. This did not occur without trade-offs, which we discuss below.

The original formal learning activity: Curriculum-based workshops. The adults have made tremendous efforts to develop engaging learning opportunities. Their original approach included consulting with teens regarding their interests, structuring formal learning activities to encompass those interests, and incorporating skill development. These took the shape of weekly workshops that involved learning skills and how to apply those to the creation of new artifacts. However, because YOUmedia is a drop-in space and has no explicit rules governing attendance, the lack of attendance became a source of frustration for the staff. One of them stated:

It can be frustrating when you think you've got a really great idea for a program, and then no teenagers show up. And it happens a lot. And it's always a challenge because you can develop something and have kids say they're gonna come, but because we're a voluntary space, there's no penalty for being absent. So that can be hard and frustrating and somewhat disheartening. Sometimes, you want to do really big projects, and it just can't come together.

Due to inconsistent attendance, staff also faced challenges implementing a curriculum across multiple sessions where the learning objectives were sequential in nature. One mentor offered, "There's a struggle right now with the curriculum because only some of it will work in this space. The kids are not required to come here as they are in school."

The addition of project-based learning opportunities. Because of some of these aforementioned struggles, staff began adding the option of project-based learning activities, for which YOUmedia partnered with external organizations. These partnerships often included incentives for teens: that they would have a chance to interact with high profile and celebrity clients. Projects, which continue to be a form of learning activity at YOUmedia, differ from curriculum-based workshops in that the needs and goals of the partner-

ing organization influence the scope of the project, the expected artifact production, and the timeline.

Through project-based activities, additional opportunities are provided to teens with existing skill sets without the requirement of a long-term commitment to workshops. These activities allow teens with advanced skills to excel in their craft, connect with established artists and other professionals, and publicize their work to larger audiences. (See "Project Based Learning Opportunities" p. 46 for examples.)

Theme-based workshops. As adults continued to struggle with engaging teens with a range of skill levels, they began offering theme-based workshops. These are shorter in duration than the traditional curriculum-based workshops, encouraging better attendance but not requiring high skills to become involved. This format is intended to engage teens in the moment, in hopes that their curiosity might be sparked and a budding interest in a particular digital or traditional medium might be cultivated. In reference to this switch, one adult stated:

I think maybe people are starting to recognize that the eight-week or six-week workshops, that model is just not going to work. But the one session, two session workshop, that seems to be working really well in this space [and] "We're gonna do this right now." Like right now, there's someone here who's engaging maybe 15 kids. Most of those kids didn't sign up, you know, but they're there and they're enjoying it right now.

As this adult suggests, given the drop-in nature of YOUmedia and the mentors' experience with attrition in the six to eight week format workshop, this modification is starting to take root. It appears to be a good option in a hybrid space.

The trade-offs that are associated with different kinds of formal learning activities at YOUmedia are summarized in **Table 3**. Overall, designing formal learning activities in the space requires staff to balance the development of appropriate programming for teens at lower skill levels, while still promoting deep engagement among teens who are building advanced skills. The

Project-Based Learning Projects

Louder than a Bomb, Brave New Voices

RONALD was interested in poetry, particularly "slam poetry," and before visiting YOUmedia was involved in the slam poetry team at his school. When he started visiting YOUmedia, he did homework, attended poetry workshops, and went to the Talent Showcase. Over time, Ronald distinguished himself at YOUmedia as one of the more proficient teen poets. He was selected by the staff to represent YOUmedia in a local teen slam poetry team competition. The team placed first and went on to compete nationally. Ronald described this event as one of his most memorable experiences.

Ronald credited YOUmedia and the staff for providing resources and opportunities to help him improve as a writer and a poet. He credits two of the staff with giving him specific critiques on poems that have helped to improve his poetry.

Ronald reported an increase in his sense of self-efficacy through meeting other highly motivated teens at YOUmedia, working with the adults in

workshops on improving his craft, and participating in "Louder than a Bomb" and "Brave New Voices." Overall, the ability to "make something happen" is a lesson he has learned at YOUmedia.

What's Going On...Now

RYAN considered himself interested in "pretty much all of the media/entertainment stuff in general." He attended a magnet elementary school with a fine arts program, where he was exposed to drama, piano, and choir. Attending programs at the YMCA and at his church further solidified his interest in music and performing arts.

Ryan considered YOUmedia a place to continue exploring these interests, particularly the record label workshop, where he had an opportunity to record some of the songs he had already composed. He spent time in the studio and learned how to use its recording devices and equipment. He learned about the What's Going On...Now project from a mentor and was intrigued by the opportunity to record and perform original material.

Ryan collaborated with a friend to complete a song for the project. Even though he was not among the few teens selected to represent YOUmedia at the Kennedy Center, Ryan's participation in this signature

project made him more confident using technology to record and produce music. He was especially pleased because he produced music that exceeded his original aspirations.

Born Brave

JADA started dabbling with Adobe Photoshop on her own to edit her pictures for school art projects. Her father, a professional photographer, noticed her interest in photography and taught her some advanced techniques with photography and film such as how to use lighting and rendering to alter images. Jada learned of YOUmedia through both a sibling and a friend. Her friend introduced her to the art staff member at YOUmedia, and she began attending his workshop on Saturdays.

Jada worked with a group of teens on the design project for Lady Gaga's Born This Way Foundation. She explains, "We designed a bus for her foundation that would tour along with her wherever she went and would help teenagers learn how to use technology for individual empowerment and help Lady Gaga spread her message of tolerance."

Along with other teens in the group, Jada had an opportunity to meet Lady Gaga and attend the launch event at Harvard for her anti-bullying initiative. It was an intense experience for Jada. She states, "I think the trip was a big life experience for me, and working with deadlines was really new...I just realized how many things could happen if I stay dedicated."

TABLE 3

Formal learning activities at YOUmedia: Design and implications

	Workshops	Projects	Theme-Based
Design	Multi-session with sequential learning goals Designed to build specific skill set	Timeline dependent on completion of project Intended to complete a specific objective	One or two session workshops Intended to engage teens around a particular theme
Implications	Higher attrition Lower engagement More opportunities for introductory skill building Fewer opportunities for advanced skill building	Lower attrition Higher engagement Fewer opportunities for introductory skill building More opportunities for advanced skill building	Lower attrition Higher engagement Almost no opportunities for introductory or advanced skill building

incentives associated with the project-based learning activities and the shorter duration of the theme-based workshops have been most successful in engaging teens at YOUmedia. However, in the project-based workshops, adults are challenged to incorporate teens at various skill levels. As one staff member stated, workshops have become less about sequential skill building and more about providing teens with unique opportunities, in terms of application of skills, and preparing them for professional media study or careers. YOUmedia staff have continuously attempted to reflect on what is and is not working for the teens in the space. Given the myriad ways in which teens interact with YOUmedia, the staff have worked towards building a repertoire of different kinds of formal learning activities in order to respond to the interests and needs of all the youth.

Tackling Ongoing Challenges

Melding the DYN and CPL cultures

As we noted earlier in this report, the hybrid nature of YOUmedia is manifest in the combination of staff members from both the DYN and CPL. The job responsibilities for staff from each of the contributing organizations were originally envisioned as distinct and separate. Library staff members were expected to carry out the day-to-day responsibilities of maintaining YOUmedia operations, such as servicing the front desk, checking out books, answering reference questions, checking out equipment, and sorting and re-shelving books. The DYN staff were charged with implementing curriculum-based workshops dedicated to building skills in a number of areas, which included poetry, graphic design, photography, and music production. This division of labor and the differences in organizational missions around learning created organizational challenges and tension among staff members as they established their professional roles and identities within a space that is constantly evolving.

In some respects, the skill sets of library staff and digital media artists at YOUmedia are complementary, allowing for a seamless integration of collaborative activities between the two organizations. One staff member even noted that textual literacies (or books) are a good foundation for digital media literacies, and the staff generally described collaborative activities as supportive of melding the two organizations in the operation of YOUmedia. She stated,

> There is a great sense of community here between the two organizations. [DYN] came in very digitally focused and [the library] came in with [their approach], but I think there was an openness there to see how we can learn from each other. What's been beautiful is...students can't necessarily tell the difference between the librarians and the DYN mentors.

However, once the library staff began to develop and implement programs, pedagogical differences emerged between the two organizations' respective approaches to teaching teens. DYN staff members were oriented towards teaching structured learning activities according to a set curriculum. As a result, the objectives of each learning activity and the products teens created were aligned with the curriculum. The library staff were oriented towards implementing engaging and enjoyable activities for teens that were not explicitly driven by any set curriculum or objectives. The support provided by each organization for teaching and mentoring teens was also different. From the beginning, DYN staff received weekly professional development from their organization that covered topics relevant to teaching digital media content and mentoring teens. The library staff did not receive weekly professional development in these areas and were unable to attend DYN's meetings because of their responsibilities for day-to-day operations in the space. One library staff member remarked,

> It's hard to plan programming while also making sure the day-to-day is happening and sometimes, as a library staff [member], we kind of get stuck on making the day-to-day work and don't have time to look at the big picture as much.

Another library staff member offered,

> I do have some difficulty keeping up with all the responsibilities...I get it done, but barely [and] by 9 o'clock, there's still more to do. I have to find ways to manage my time to mentor teens, work on workshops, and then also work on library focused things.

Staff members from both organizations identified differences in teaching teens as an area requiring further alignment to harmonize the ways individuals develop curriculum, deliver content, and structure formal learning activities. As a result, CPL staff was incorporated into some DYN professional development sessions. Additionally, a weekly meeting for YOUmedia staff was created to focus on professional development specific to their roles in YOUmedia and on improving communication across the two organizations.

Building skills versus engaging youth: A conundrum. As outlined above, teens always have the choice to pursue recreational and social activities at YOUmedia (e.g., hanging out with friends, playing video games, or surfing the internet). In this context, adults have to design appealing learning activities, considering the trade-offs between skill development and keeping teens engaged regardless of their skill level. Sometimes staff members leverage their relationships with teens to encourage participation in structured learning activities, and their relationships allow the adults to nudge occasionally without coming across as overbearing.

One staff member states, "These teens are not just going to sign up for a workshop because you're cool, especially when you're competing with Rock Band or something like that." Yet, the nudging does not necessarily lead to the commitment teens need to demonstrate to develop skills or take advantage of the signature projects.

This conundrum emerges from having as much teen choice as a hybrid context allows while also delivering an interest-driven learning program. Our data show that, when given the choice, only about one-quarter of teens utilize the resources within YOUmedia to create digital products and take advantage of opportunities to showcase or perform their work. These teens tend to have modest or advanced levels of skill in digital media creation already, and they come to YOUmedia primarily because the space offers activities that help enrich what they already do well. Most teens, on the other hand, are inclined to socialize and use the resources at YOUmedia for digital media consumption rather than creation. They may dabble in structured learning activities at the suggestion of a peer or adult. However, they may not consistently remain engaged with these activities to "level up" or build skills that will enable them to take advantage of higher-profile learning opportunities at YOUmedia. (An exception to this is the group of teens who use the recording studio. They are willing to

complete the required workshops to become certified to have access to the recording studio.)

Here is the conundrum: Privileging teen choice seems to incentivize the teens with more ambition and advanced production skills, who navigate their way more often to the high-profile learning opportunities. Because most teens who are novices do not reach advanced levels of skill, they are unable to take advantage of the opportunities such skill affords for participating in signature projects.

We recognize that, in any activity, the most motivated participants are going to gain more. Yet it is important to raise the following question: Can the degree of teen choice be modified to encourage more commitment and consistency from teens who are less inclined to participate in structured learning activities while also retaining the sense of freedom many teens appreciate about YOUmedia? YOUmedia affirms teens' independence by giving them the option to socialize in a safe, friendly environment. Potential considerations to incorporate more structure and broaden the effect of YOUmedia's learning activities will have to be weighed against preserving the important element of choice.

Maintenance of equipment and other issues. Several staff members identified challenges related to the technological resources at YOUmedia, an area of difficulty also highlighted by staff in our one year report. The subject of equipment maintenance is still an issue that staff members have to troubleshoot regularly. One YOUmedia staff member remarked, "Teenagers break stuff really quickly. Really, really quickly. And it is a big concern on how often we can replace the equipment." As indicated in our previous report,[37] staff members successfully implemented educational processes such as studio certification, whereby teen users of the recording studio have to undergo a formal training prior to utilizing this space without supervision. YOUmedia staff also described being more vigilant about conducting a daily inventory to assess whether laptop computers and other equipment are functioning properly. The staff implemented some preventative processes to decrease the incidences of broken equipment, but many contend they might never be able to fully curtail the issue.

Other technological challenges proved to be more formidable, affecting the ability of staff to be nimble and fluid while teaching teens. One YOUmedia staff member reported, "We're restricted to using Safari right now on Macs and only using the public browser on Windows, which makes it really difficult when I am trying to do certain [activities] with the kids." YOUmedia staff also cited the lack of administrative access to make hardware or software changes on computers as an obstacle to running the workshops. These challenges affected adults' ability to troubleshoot general issues with computers and also forced them to revamp or entirely eliminate workshop sessions. One staff member explained,

I try and do some upkeep on the laptops although with the tech department the way that it is in CPL, they have everything locked down extremely tight. So what that means for me is looking at the laptop, quickly diagnosing that I can't do anything to fix it because of the administrative password and then just calling tech services and they take a look at it.

Another staff member explained the difficulty around the lack of administrative access, "If we need to install a program or install anything to do a workshop, we can't do it...If you're trying to do something on the fly, you can't do it." Without administrative access and the ability to install software or make other changes to computers, YOUmedia staff are solely reliant upon the IT department at HWLC to resolve technological issues of this nature. However, the IT department is also responsible for providing support to the entire library, which affects the timeliness in which they can resolve issues with YOUmedia equipment.

Balancing change and constancy. The challenges of melding two organizational cultures and maintaining technology emerged over the course of YOUmedia's implementation and have been ongoing. As demonstrated above, staff members working in this innovative context have some latitude in enacting practices, protocols, and procedures to mitigate these challenges. Their efforts also signify attempts to instantiate structure in a fluid organizational environment that privileges adaptability and responsiveness at times (such as when staff members take on new roles) and consistency at other times (such as ensuring the availability and usability of technological equipment at YOUmedia). We ended our data collection at a time when a new library commissioner had been appointed to take the helm of all libraries in Chicago. The new commissioner is committed to YOUmedia's sustainability, setting aside funds in the overall library budget for operating expenses at YOUmedia. In addition, he has recruited six teen/young adult services librarians for HWLC and branch libraries with YOUmedias. These librarians have special training in young adult literature, youth driven technology, media literacy for youth, and teens' learning networks. The shift in leadership creates the opportunity to seek a reasonable balance between change and innovation on the one hand and constancy and organizational capacity on the other hand. It will be important to continue to create structures and processes for operating YOUmedia effectively. These include means of communication across the staff and, particularly, across the partner organizations. As DYN reduces its role over time, the new teen/young adult librarians will need to assume the multifaceted mentor role. In addition, there is a need for time for planning and for tracking youth attendance and activity. Finally, the staff needs to establish processes for preparing the equipment for projects, as well as for replacing and repairing equipment. As previously noted, the absence of certain concrete structures has prevented operations from running smoothly.

CHAPTER 5

Interpretive Summary and Considerations for Practice

The founders of YOUmedia aspired to create a digital media-infused learning center in Chicago's central library that would attract teens to come and hang out, make videos, write poetry, compose music, and explore other art forms.

They hoped teens would pursue their interests, using library resources, guidance from adults, and the synergy of other teens being involved in similar pursuits to develop their skills in digital media arts and their capacity for self-expression. They wanted teens to create products and to perform in the context of a safe, welcoming, and stimulating environment.

We estimate that YOUmedia attracts between 350 and 500 teens each week. They come from a wide swath of Chicago, particularly from the south and southeast sides. These teens have arrived at YOUmedia mainly through word of mouth; little outreach was needed. Although about one-quarter of the young people attend nearby schools, others need to make a special trip to participate. In fact, regardless of where they go to school, 80 percent of the teens live five miles or more away from the library. YOUmedia teens persist in their attendance; over half have been coming for more than a year.

YOUmedia serves a fairly heterogeneous population, with teens who attend a variety of high schools, and even some homeschooled teens. The group is somewhat higher achieving than the overall CPS high school population. Thirty-five percent attend a selective enrollment high school compared to the CPS average of 10 percent. This is notable because students and teachers in selective enrollment schools use technology for teaching and learning more than students and teachers in neighborhood or charter schools (**see companion**

report, **The Use of Technology in Chicago Public Schools 2011: Perspectives from Students, Teachers, and Principals**[38]). Whether it was due to their school or their own habits, about one-third of the teens came to YOUmedia with digital media experience, already having created blogs, games, songs, and multi-media products.

YOUmedia has been particularly successful in attracting African American males, many of whom use the music recording studio. They comprise about 40 percent of all teens in the space, while making up 22 percent of CPS high school students. It is encouraging to see these teens involved at YOUmedia because historically African American males have been underserved by out-of-school programs.[39]

The combination of the physical space, the staff, and an environment that is accepting but also encourages exploration has yielded a deep sense of community among most participants. The vast majority of teens feel that they are an important part of the community and that it is cool to be excited about their interests. Some teens expressed that they felt more accepted at YOUmedia than at school; others said it was a good "nerd hangout."

Because the space is a fluid hybrid of both unstructured and structured activities, teens can choose their interests and the intensity with which to pursue them. This gives them a kind of autonomy that is different from school and different from many other out-of

-school programs. Teens expressed fervent appreciation for this autonomy, perhaps because they do not encounter it in many other places.

This hybrid design, which essentially brings teens' learning and social worlds together, has a profound influence on the ways in which teens participate. What they do varies considerably. For the majority of teens, YOUmedia meets a need for a place to relax, socialize, read, and do homework—all positive uses of the library. A minority of teens, mainly those we classified as Creators, produce products and perform—music, poetry, videos, graphic designs, and critiques of peers' work. They also collaborate on signature events like designing Lady Gaga's bus or remixing Marvin Gaye's songs.

Clearly, those teens who invested the most time and effort also claimed the most benefits. Seventy-five to 85 percent of the Creators reported spillover benefits from YOUmedia in terms of improved writing, schoolwork, and ability to communicate with adults. Compared with teens who participated in other ways, the Creators had the largest percentage reporting improvements in their media arts skills. However, it is noteworthy that a substantial fraction of youth who fall into the other four participation categories also claimed benefits. Even among the Socializers, 40 to 50 percent of the youth thought YOUmedia helped their academic skills.

YOUmedia largely fulfilled the founders' desires to offer teens a comfortable and stimulating place to regularly hang out and pursue their interests, along with like-minded peers and adults. What was less obvious at YOUmedia's inception was that allowing participants the choice of participating intensely or not had consequences on the different types of outcomes YOUmedia could realize. The founders wanted teens to use library resources; the teens we classified as Readers/Studiers did indeed do this, checking out books and using the computers and internet to complete their school assignments.

The founders also hoped to move teens to develop greater expertise in their art form. While those we classified as Floaters and Experimenters used the human and digital resources available to them, they did not move toward increased expertise in any measurable way. However, the Creators made the most discernible progress toward gaining expertise in their chosen arena.

While YOUmedia might not have completely fulfilled its founders' aspirations for turning teen interest into teen expertise, at a time when public high schools are struggling to engage students in their classes, it is significant that YOUmedia has been able to engage almost one-quarter of the teens intensively in production and performance (the Creators). Our findings suggest that the bright physical design of YOUmedia and the lure of digital media tools by themselves are not sufficient to capture youths' commitment to learn new skills. Instead, teens get involved because staff members spark their interests, teach them how to develop their art, encourage and counsel them, connect them to opportunities, and showcase their products. At the same time, teens share interests with their peers. It is the combination of relationships with peers and adults, learning experiences, opportunities to be creative, and the digital tools that is critical.

These characteristics of the YOUmedia learning environment lead us to further discussion of Connected Learning.

Connected Learning Model

In the Introduction, we considered the key principles of learning that Ito and her colleagues recently set forth: The Connected Learning Model. These authors drew on prior research and the recent experiences of practitioners (including those at YOUmedia) who have been experimenting with digital media activities to promote interest-driven learning. Previous research has shown that the most effective learning occurs when the student has a strong interest in the topic, has social support in pursuing the learning tasks, and receives recognition for accomplishments.[40]

Building on this research, Connected Learning attempts to bring together three spheres of learning that are often disconnected with each other in young people's lives: interests, peer culture, and academic content (**see Figure 15**). The framework recognizes that when teens are interested in a topic, they are much more likely to acquire knowledge and expertise in that area. Connected Learning also calls for learners to be connected socially—teens with their peers and with adults. In such a context, youth contribute, share, and give feedback to one another. Interest-driven activities and peer culture can be oriented toward academic achievement, career opportunity, and civic engagement. In other words, learning activities may support academic learning or enlighten teens' understanding of future opportunities, or provide an outlet for community involvement. Ito and her colleagues also argue that digital media amplifies the opportunities for Connected Learning, but such learning does not always involve digital media.[41]

Connected learning joins three spheres[42]

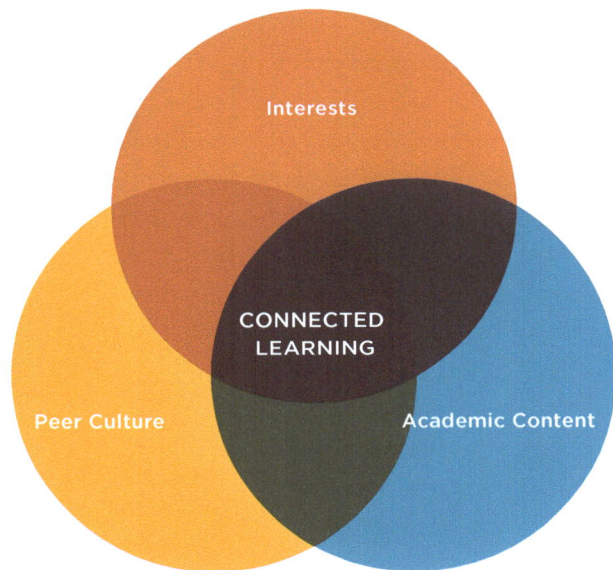

The Connected Learning Model was developed well after UChicago CCSR undertook this study of YOUmedia. Yet given the recent publication of *Connected Learning: An Agenda for Research and Design*[43] and the ongoing interest in and consideration of the model by researchers and practitioners through such means as the website connect-edlearning.tv, it is worthwhile to reflect on the evidence we found of Connected Learning at YOUmedia Chicago.

Clearly, many YOUmedia participants experience some parts of Connected Learning, but the Creators are most likely to experience all the elements. More specifically, we observed the following:

- While the vast majority of YOUmedia teens know that it is cool to be excited about their interests and that they share interests with peers and staff, the proportion who worked with an adult frequently on a project was generally small. The exception was the Creators,

among whom almost one-half worked with a staff member frequently.

- A portion of YOUmedia teens already had interests when they began coming to YOUmedia, with the Creators most likely to have them. Most teens also developed new interests while there. However, a limiting factor for some teens in pursuing their interests was their flagging motivation to participate in skill-building workshops and projects.

- Relatively large percentages of youth seemed to perceive the links between YOUmedia activities and academic achievement. They believed YOUmedia helped to improve their schoolwork, their writing, and their ability to communicate with adults. A large percentage also reported that at YOUmedia they learned about opportunities after high school.

- However, only a small group of teens were able to contribute to the high profile events that would reflect well on them and perhaps open up future opportunities for academic achievement or career success. These included teens who displayed art at the Contemporary Museum of Art, won the What's Going On...Now competition, and worked on the design of the bus for Lady Gaga's Born This Way Foundation.

Strengthening the environment to support Connected Learning. Just as they embraced Ito's earlier ideas of hanging out, messing around, and geeking out, the YOUmedia staff has begun to articulate the Connected Learning framework.

From what the teens told us, YOUmedia Chicago is doing well in making teens' interests central to its programming. Youth indicated that there is a strong ethos that is supportive of teens pursuing their passions, and large fractions of them reported that the staff members introduced them to new interests and that over time relatively more of them were working on their interests.

In addition, social connections between teens, their peers, and the adults appear quite healthy in the physical space. Teens were extremely positive about the welcoming environment and the value of the staff. However, the online space has not been as successful as a way to encourage socializing and friendships among teens. At the same time, the staff and Remix Learning have come to the conclusion that the site may support learning activities related to workshops and projects better than casual social networking. Other learning laboratories should think carefully about the purpose of an online network.

YOUmedia Chicago has not been as systematic as it could be about the links between learning activities and academic, career, and civic engagement opportunities. We observed such linkages on occasion, particularly related to the special events and partnership activities, like What's Going On...Now. It may encourage teens who aspire to be Creators or to pursue careers in such fields as music and photography to have a clear articulation of the paths to expertise and opportunities that may be available in the future. Furthermore, teens need to realize that there are different levels of expertise and that reaching for more advanced levels will lead to interesting opportunities for them in terms of academics, career interests, or civic engagement.

Is it possible to get more teens to experience Connected Learning? Increasing the proportion of youth who produce and perform and experience the full complement of Connected Learning experiences is, first, the age-old question of how to persuade more teens to get more deeply involved. It was challenging for staff to design structured learning activities that could attract teens to learn new skills in the face of teen choice to spend time socializing or messing around. Because teens may or may not stick with a planned curriculum, the staff cannot work with them to develop skills needed to participate in the more advanced projects. Yet if teens do not develop their skills, it will be difficult for youth to produce and perform.

But increasing the proportion of youth who produce or perform is also a question of staffing. Connected Learning experiences require working with peers and adults, which has implications for staff burden. More staff time is needed not only to serve more teens but also to develop relationships and manage partnerships with artists like Toni Morrison. Junior mentors, who have been appointed by YOUmedia in the past, could extend the staff capacity somewhat.

Considerations for Practice

In view of our aim to provide a knowledge base that will be useful to the YOUmedia leaders in Chicago and leaders of learning laboratories across the country, we discuss below considerations for practice.

Sustaining the partnership and building organizational capacity. YOUmedia Chicago was created

through a specific partnership; its particular strengths and challenges reflect the beliefs, philosophies, and working relationships formed over time. Each party contributed its core expertise, competence, and resources. In the year one report, we documented the accomplishment of the creation of YOUmedia through the partnership among the MacArthur Foundation, DYN, CPL, and the Pearson Foundation. During the last three years, DYN and CPL have operated the program together. They have succeeded in attracting a large clientele of teens who appreciate the program and report multiple benefits from attending it. Nonetheless, stresses and tensions are inevitable when two organizations function together as the operating agent. YOUmedia Chicago and other learning laboratories created by partnerships need to think and plan carefully so that they can develop governance and operational structures to implement their programs effectively. In fact, prior studies have established that the out-of-school programs that succeed in getting youth to sustain their participation provide for frequent and regular staff meetings.[44]

Another aspect of organizational capacity is systematic collection of data to gauge the success of new efforts and inform strategies moving forward. One basic data element that is needed is attendance. In part, due to the fact that there were two entrances to YOUmedia and that it is a drop-in center where teens can freely come and go, it was difficult to collect attendance consistently. However, this made it problematic to determine the size and characteristics of the population served by YOUmedia and to ascertain whether youth who participated frequently gained more benefits than those who did not. The research team used a combination of censuses, surveys, and interviews to gather this information, but this is expensive and not practical for the program. Thus, YOUmedia and other learning laboratories should establish procedures to track participation. It would also be worthwhile to track other indicators of valued activity as well—for example, who is producing artifacts, performing, or checking out books.

A convenient location pays off. YOUmedia Chicago benefits greatly from being in a central location near public transportation. As we showed, even youth living five miles away or more can get to YOUmedia easily.

Also, it is located at street level where passersby can see the activities through the large windows.

The size of the space matters. YOUmedia Chicago is large—more than 5,000 square feet. Most other programs are not likely to have such ample space and will have to select carefully the programming and curriculum they can successfully offer.

Adequate funding for acquiring and maintaining equipment and software is a must. With the heavy reliance on digital equipment, YOUmedia Chicago and other organizations need to ensure that the equipment and software works and that they are updated regularly.

A practical toolkit for launching a learning laboratory. The YOUmedia Network provides a website and an online community for organizations wishing to establish a YOUmedia or a learning laboratory. It offers information and guidance on everything from the physical space and programming to a sample budget. For more information, visit http://www.youmedia.org/toolkit.

Future Research

A clear limitation of this study is that it is primarily based on self-reported data. Initially we had hoped to have accurate YOUmedia attendance data that could be linked to school data and other out-of-school program data through CitySpan, a citywide database on out-of-school programs. However, this database was not sufficiently complete to use for research purposes. While we learned a great deal from the perceptions of teens and staff, systematic data about participants would have added to our knowledge. A productive next step would be to develop performance measures of the outcomes that the Connected Learning Model has begun to define—academic benefits, career interests, and civic engagement. This could help answer how extensive learning may be. In addition, it would be valuable to follow participants over time to understand long-term consequences, if any, of participating in programs like YOUmedia.

Broader Considerations

In many respects, YOUmedia appears to have succeeded at what it set out to do. Without much outreach effort, YOUmedia attracted a large group of teens, most of whom reported that they attend regularly and frequently.

These young people consider YOUmedia to be an interesting and stimulating place where they can hang out with friends, work on school assignments, or pursue an interest with friends and staff. This is especially important because YOUmedia has substantially increased the number of teens who come to HWLC.

It is also significant that these opportunities are provided by CPL at no cost to the youth. Recent evidence has shown that upper-income families invest far more than lower-income families in enrichment activities for their children, and the gap is rapidly widening between the two classes.[45] Thus positive opportunities at no cost for Chicago youth, most of whom are eligible for free and reduced price lunch, are laudable.

YOUmedia may have fallen short of expectations in two areas. One was the efficacy of YOUmedia Online in providing a platform that was easy to use and extended the learning opportunities beyond the space. The other was the proportion of youth (about one-quarter) who developed deep expertise in their specialized areas. Should we expect more teens to be writing poetry, working on the magazine, producing videos, making music, etc.? In view of the fact that another quarter of the teens work on their schoolwork, about half the youth were productively engaged. The others were hanging out and socializing, but they also were getting exposure to a variety of activities. Given the multiple aspirations for the space and reports by teens of benefits received, perhaps it is unrealistic to expect more.

YOUmedia's experience suggests that the Connected Learning Model holds promise for an approach to learning that takes advantage of teens' interests and the availability of digital media. The approach is relevant to schools as well. Recall that teens become engaged in their projects through the combination of relationships and learning experiences in a well-designed and equipped environment. Beyond the brief introduction we provided to Connected Learning, Ito and her colleagues have developed concrete design principles for implementing the approach.[46]

Simultaneous to conducting this study of YOUmedia Chicago, the authors also investigated the use of technology in CPS. There has been gradual progress in incorporating technology into the curriculum. Yet on average, only about half of high school students were using technology at least once a week for completing their assignments. Technology was used rarely or never by 20 to 30 percent.[47] This stands in stark contrast to the competence, energy, and creativity of the teens we observed at YOUmedia. Especially in the current era of slim budgets, opportunities exist to capitalize on digital networks and online resources to offer learning experiences that engage teens. Almost all youth (92 percent of sixth- to twelfth-graders in CPS) have access to the internet at home.[48] With its focus on interest-driven learning, YOUmedia supplements the educational experiences of the teens who attend, but it also provides an example to the broader education community of activities that motivate and engage urban youth.

References

Austin, K., Ehrlich, S., Puckett, C., and Singleton, J. with Sporte, S.E., Sebring, P.B., Nacu, D.C., and Brown, E. (2011)
YOUmedia Chicago: Reimagining Learning, Literacies, and Libraries, A Snapshot of Year 1. Chicago: University of Chicago Consortium on Chicago School Research.

Bushweller, K.C. (2012)
The Pace of Change Quickens. *Education Week, 31* (23): S2. Available online at http://www.edweek.org/ew/articles/2012/03/07/23biz-overview. h31.html (accessed on July 29, 2012).

Cohen, C. and Kahne, J. (2012)
Participatory Politics: New Media and Youth Political Action. http://ypp.dmlcentral.net/sites/all/files/publications/YPP_Survey_Report_FULL.pdf (accessed on July 24, 2012).

Deschenes, S.N., Arbreton, A., Little, P.M., Herrera, C., Grossman, J.B., and Weiss, H.B. (2010)
Engaging Older Youth: Program and City-Level Strategies to Support Sustained Participation in Out-of-School Time. Cambridge, MA: Harvard Family Research Project.

Deschenes, S.N., McDonald, M., and McLaughlin, M. (2004)
Youth Organizations: From Principles to Practice. In S.F. Hamilton and M.A. Hamilton (Eds.) *The Youth Development Handbook: Coming of Age in American Communities.* Thousand Oaks, CA: Sage.

Duncan, G.J. and Murnane, R. (2011)
Whither Opportunity? Rising Inequality, Schools, and Children's Life Chances. New York, NY: Russell Sage.

Ehrlich, S.B., Sporte, S.E., and Sebring, P.B. (Forthcoming)
The Use of Technology in the Chicago Public Schools: Perspectives from Students, Teachers, and Principals. Chicago: University of Chicago.

Fashiola, O.S. (2003)
Developing the Talents of African American Male Students During the Nonschool Hours. *Urban Education, 38* (4): 398-430. Available online at http://uex.sagepub.com/content/38/4/398 (accessed on November 29, 2012).

Gallagher, L. (2008)
Assessing Youth Impact of the Computer Clubhouse Network. Menlo Park, CA: Center for Technology in Learning. SRI International. Available at http://www.computerclubhouse.org/sites/default/files/CapstoneReportFinal.pdf (accessed January 21, 2013).

Hannon, V. (2007)
'Next Practice' in Education: A Disciplined Approach to Innovation. Available online at http://www.innovation-unit. org/sites/default/files/Next%20Practice%20in%20Education.pdf (accessed on July 29, 2012).

Herr-Stephenson, B., Rhoten, D., Perkel, D., and Sims, C. (2011)
Digital Media and Technology in Afterschool Programs, Libraries, and Museums. Cambridge: MIT Press.

Ito, M. et al. (2009)
Hanging Out, Messing Around, and Geeking Out: Kids Living and Learning with New Media. Cambridge, MA: MIT Press.

Ito, M., Gutierrez, K., Livingston, S., Penuel, W., Rhodes, J., Salen, K., Schor, J., Watkins, S.C., Sefton-Green, J., and Watkins, C. (2013)
Connected Learning: An Agenda for Research and Design. Irvine, CA: Digital Media and Learning Research Hub.

Lee, A. (December 12, 2012)
Personal communication.

Lee, A. (January 14, 2013)
Personal communication.

National Center for Education Statistics (2012)
National Assessment of Educational Progress: NAEP Technology and Engineering Literacy (TEL) Assessment. Available online at http://nces.ed.gov/nationalreport-card/techliteracy/ (accessed on August 10, 2012).

National Governors Association Center for Best Practices, Council of Chief State School Officers (2010)
Common Core State Standards (English Language Arts Literacy). Available online at http://www.Corestandards.org/the-standards/english-language-arts-standards/introduction/students-who-are-college-and-career-ready-in-reading-writing-speaking-listening-and-language/ (accessed December 1, 2012).

Patton, M.Q. (2011)
Developmental Evaluation: Applying Complexity Concepts to Enhance Innovation and Use. New York: The Guilford Press.

Roderick, M., Nagaoka, J., Coca, V., Moeller, E. with Roddie, K., Gilliam, J., and Patton, D. (2008)
From High School to the Future: Potholes on the Road to College. Chicago: University of Chicago Consortium on Chicago School Research.

Shelly, G.B., Cashman, T.J., Gunter, G.A., and Gunter, R.E. (2007)
Teachers Discovering Computers: Integrating Technology and Digital Media in the Classroom (5th Edition). Florence, KY: Course Technology, Cengage Learning.

Strobel, K., and Kirshner, B., O'Donoghue, J., and Wallin McLaughlin, M. (2008)
Qualities that Attract Urban Youth to After-school Settings and Promote Continued Participation. *The Teachers College Record, 110*(8), 1677-1705.

The White House, Office of the Press Secretary (September 16, 2010)
President Obama to Announce Major Expansion of "Educate to Innovate" Campaign to Improve Science, Technology, Engineering and Math (STEM) Education. Available online at http://www.whitehouse.gov/the-press-office/2010/09/16/president-obama-announce-major-expansion-educate-innovate-campaign-impro (accessed on November 23, 2010).

Appendix A
Data Collection Activities and Research Methods

The research team actively collected data from January 2010 through June 2012. These data included observations of activities in YOUmedia; interviews of teens, staff, and leaders; and surveys of teens. The lead field researcher spent considerable time and was "embedded" at YOUmedia about half-time starting at the end of 2010 and going through June 2012.

Data collected during the first year formed the basis for the year one report, *YOUmedia Chicago: Reimagining Learning, Literacies, and Libraries: A Snapshot of Year 1*. Data collected in years two and three are included in the current report. These data were collected for a variety of analytic purposes. First, observations of YOUmedia's formal and informal activities allowed researchers to understand its ongoing operation at HWLC, learn how teens behave when there, and describe teens' production activities. These observations were enhanced by informal interactions with teens meant to gather unobservable information (e.g., teens' motivations, and the successes and challenges they experienced while producing or consuming media).

Second, formal interviews allowed researchers to deeply understand YOUmedia from a variety of perspectives. Formal interviews of teens provided a lens into their experiences. Interviews of staff provided insight into their perceptions of the design of formal activities and the ways in which they worked with teens, YOUmedia's impact on teens, and the challenges they encountered with YOUmedia as an organization. Interviewing the leadership helped researchers understand the history, development, and design of YOUmedia along with its successes and challenges.

Finally, collecting survey data allowed a broader picture of teen experience at YOUmedia. The surveys were intended to gauge the following about teens: (1) personal characteristics; (2) technological characteristics; (3) engagement with YOUmedia; (4) perceived benefits; and (5) development of interests. **Table 4** provides an indication of when these data were collected.

TABLE 4

Data collection activities

Activity	Year 1		Year 2			Year 3		
	2010	2010	2010	2011	2011	2011	2012	2012
	Jan-Apr	May-Aug	Sep-Dec	Jan-Apr	May-Aug	Sep-Dec	Jan-Apr	May-Aug
Observations-Unstructured[1]	x	x	x	X	x	x	x	x
Unstructured interviews, youth and YM HWLC Staff[2]	x	x	x	X	x	x	x	x
Interviews-Structured								
• Youth (not case-study)		20						
• Youth (case-study)					20	14		19
• YM HWLC Staff[2]		15			8		10	10
• Leadership[3]		8				4		6
Census of Youth					362		501	
Survey of Youth					180		243	

1 Two-hour observations for 3 to 4 days/week from 3 to 8 pm
2 YOUmedia Harold Washington Library Center Staff includes adult mentors, librarians, and security guards
3 Leaders of the MacArthur Foundation, Chicago Public Library, and Digital Youth Network

Research Methods —
Years Two and Three

Observations at HWLC

Members of the research team visited YOUmedia at HWLC three or four times a week between the hours of 3 and 8 pm. Each visit lasted about two hours. They observed structured and informal activities and conducted informal interviews with staff and teens. During workshops and other structured activities, researchers were non-participant observers who documented events as they happened by taking notes and making audio recordings. During informal activities, researchers were participant observers who interacted with teens.

Observers kept detailed field notes from each visit. Field notes were transcribed, and some were coded using Atlas.ti. Codes were based on researchers' observations and the goals identified by YOUmedia's leadership. Each of three researchers was responsible for a category of similar codes. After 15 field notes were coded, researchers summarized them in a report. These reports were then reviewed to identify patterns and themes.

Interviews
Case-Study Teens

In spring 2011, researchers asked staff members to recommend teens who were different from each other in their patterns of attendance; their personal characteristics (gender, race/ethnicity, grade level in school, and type of school they attend); and/or the types of activities they participate in at YOUmedia (hanging out with friends, using digital media tools, attending workshops, creating projects, posting projects online, and/or commenting on others' projects). Twenty-six teens were recommended. Researchers explained the research project to each of them and gave them the opportunity to participate. Of the 26 teens, 23 agreed to participate. Before the first interview was conducted, each of these teens completed assent forms and their parents completed consent forms. Two of the non-participants never received the consent of their parents, and one declined to participate because of time constraints.

See Table 5 for the personal characteristics of the 23 teens in the case-study sample.

TABLE 5

Characteristics of the case-study sample

GENDER	
Female	13
Male	10
CPS SCHOOL TYPE	
Selective Enrollment	7
Charter	6
Neighborhood	4
Home Schooled	2
Career Academy	2
Other (Military, Alternative)	2
RACE/ETHNICITY	
Black/African American	12
White/Caucasian	5
Latino/a	3
Asian	1
Bi-racial/Multi-racial	2
GRADE	
Ninth Grade	6
Tenth Grade	9
Eleventh Grade	7
Twelfth Grade	1

Semi-structured interviews were conducted in waves, with each using a protocol that was similar but not identical in content to the others. Seventeen of these teens were interviewed all three times, and an additional five were interviewed once. One teen was not interviewed at all.

Staff Members and Leadership

Researchers interviewed all staff members from CPL and DYN on three occasions during years two and three. Leaders from the MacArthur Foundation, CPL, and DYN were interviewed twice. The interviews were semi-structured, and each used a protocol that was similar, but not identical, in content to the others.

Interviews — Coding and Data Analysis

All interviews were transcribed verbatim and coded using Atlas.ti. Researchers used both inductive and deductive approaches to develop codes. The first codes mirrored the interview protocol; multiple researchers used them to code the same interviews. Inter-rater reliability was checked by comparing codes across researchers. Areas where researchers disagreed were used to refine and add codes and to generate a final list of codes. Each interview was then coded using the final coding scheme with each of three researchers being responsible for a set of similar codes.

After all interviews were coded, codes were summarized across interviews. Researchers (1) created descriptive summaries for each code that showed details of responses and (2) searched for patterns in the ways respondents were connected across various themes.

Teen Census and Surveys

Summer 2011

From July 11, 2011, through July 23, 2011, researchers collected survey data at HWLC. From Monday, July 11, through Saturday, July 16 (Friday excluded), researchers took a census of the teens visiting HWLC. The purpose was to develop an estimate of the YOUmedia population by counting the number of teens visiting YOUmedia during a week and by gathering background information about them. Background information included the major demographic characteristics of the teens: (1) age, (2) gender, (3) race/ethnicity, (4) last grade in school, and (5) type of school attended in previous school year. During YOUmedia's busiest times, researchers approached each unique teen in the space and asked him or her to complete a questionnaire that had five items. The survey was paper-based and completed anonymously.

From July 18 through July 23 (Friday excluded), researchers administered a questionnaire to teens at YOUmedia. The online questionnaire was administered anonymously and was administered on the same days of the week and times of day as the census. Researchers approached most teens visiting HWLC during the specified time period and asked them to complete the survey. As an incentive to participate, researchers offered teens a $5 gift card to a local sandwich shop.

The questionnaire was completed by 98 percent of the respondents at HWLC and 2 percent (5) at another location.

Other than type of school, the background characteristics of the teens responding to the questionnaire were statistically the same as those of the teens in the census. The percentage of teens attending college was larger in the census than in the survey.

Spring 2012

From March 12, 2012, through April 4, 2012, researchers collected survey data at HWLC. From Monday, March 12, through Saturday, March 17 (Friday excluded), researchers took a census of the teens visiting HWLC. As with the first census, this census was intended to estimate the population by counting the number of teens visiting YOUmedia during a week, and gathering background information about them. The procedures were the same as those used in July 2011.

From Monday, March 19, through Wednesday, April 4 (Fridays and Sundays excluded), researchers administered a questionnaire to teens at YOUmedia. The procedures used were the same as those used in the survey of summer 2011. Again, as an incentive to participate, researchers offered youth a $5 gift card to a local sandwich shop. The survey was completed by 96 percent of the respondents at HWLC and 4 percent (10) at another location.

Chi square tests indicated that, other than type of school, the background characteristics of the teens responding to the survey were statistically the same as those of the teens in the census. Differences between census- and survey-takers were the following: 16 percent of census-takers versus 13 percent of survey respondents attended charter schools; five percent versus 3 percent attended private schools; three percent versus 9 percent were home schooled. To see the survey instruments, visit https://ccsr.uchicago.edu/sites/default/files/publications/2012YOUmediaSurvey.pdf

Appendix B
Travel Patterns of Teens

Researchers used results from two items on the 2012 teen survey to calculate the probable travel pattern of each teen to and from YOUmedia at HWLC.

• What is the name of your school?

• What is the zip code of your primary home?

Researchers made the following assumptions to complete this analysis:

• Teens who completed the survey on a weekday travelled to the HWLC from school and then travelled from HWLC to their home.

• Teens who completed the survey on a weekend travelled to the HWLC from home and then travelled from HWLC back to their home.

• When travelling either to or from the HWLC, a teen's modes of transportation included walking, riding the bus, taking the "L," and/or taking the Metra.

• When traveling either to or from YOUmedia, a teen chose the mode of transportation that required the least amount of walking to and from that mode of transportation.

• Teens who either attend school or live within a mile of HWLC were classified as "downtown anyway."

• Teens who attend school throughout the city and whose mode of transportation takes them through downtown were classified as "on the way home from school."

• Teens who were neither "downtown anyway" nor "on the way home from school" were those who made a deliberate trip to HWLC and were classified as "special trip."

Fourteen percent of teens completed the survey on a weekend. These teens were classified as "special trip" because they were assumed to make a round trip from their home to the HWLC and then directly back home. Information about these teens is summarized in the table below.

TABLE 6

Travel patterns of weekend participants

	Percent of Teens
Residence-Section of Chicago	
South/Southeast	70%
Other-Various	30%
Home to HWLC-Distance	
5 or Fewer Miles	23%
6 through 10 Miles	60%
11 through 15 Miles	17%
Transportation-Round Trip	
"L"	70%
Metra	23%
Bus	7%

Eighty-six percent of teens completed the survey on a weekday. These teens were classified in one of the three categories depending upon the assumed modes of transportation both to and from YOUmedia.

TABLE 7

Travel patterns of weekday participants

	Downtown Anyway (Percent of Teens)	On Way Home from School (Percent of Teens)	Special Trip (Percent of Teens)
School-Section of Chicago			
Downtown	94%	0%	0%
South/Southeast	0%	22%	62%
North/Northwest	2%	44%	14%
West	2%	22%	11%
Southwest	2%	12%	13%
School to HWLC-Distance			
5 or Fewer Miles	98%	89%	56%
6 through 10 Miles	2%	11%	26%
11+ Miles	0%	0%	18%
Transportation-School to HWLC			
"L"	6%	76%	47%
Metra	0%	0%	12%
Bus	0%	9%	26%
"L" and Bus	0%	15%	15%
Walk	94%	0%	0%
Residence-Section of Chicago			
South/Southeast	39%	48%	61%
West	0%	9%	15%
Southwest	24%	24%	11%
North/Northwest	28%	19%	13%
Downtown	9%	0%	0%
Home to HWLC-Distance			
5 or Fewer Miles	17%	19%	26%
6 through 10 Miles	52%	57%	53%
11+ Miles	31%	24%	21%
Transportation-HWLC to Home			
"L"	41%	59%	68%
Metra	15%	15%	22%
Bus	7%	4%	3%
"L" and Bus	28%	22%	7%
Walk	9%	0%	0%

Appendix C
Supplementary Tables and Graphs

TABLE 8

Chapter 3: Most YOUmedia Teens Travel from and to the South Side		
School Location	Home Location	Percent of Teens
South Side	South Side	58%
West Side	West Side	10%
Southwest Side	Southwest Side	9%
North Side	North Side	7%
Other	Other	16%

Source: 2012 YOUmedia Survey

TABLE 9

Chapter 3: A Third of YOUmedia Teens Said They Have a Female Guardian with at Least a College Degree	
Educational Level	Percent of Teens
4-Year or Graduate Degree	38%
2-Year Degree or Some College	25%
HS Diploma or Less	31%
Don't Know/Other	6%

Source: 2012 YOUmedia Survey

TABLE 10

Chapter 3: Many YOUmedia Teens Say They Were Using Digital Media before Visiting YOUmedia	
Create a(an)...	Percent of Teens
Blog Post	39%
Original Video or Song	39%
Original Website	24%
Original Graphic Design	26%
Post Original Work Online	56%
Give Feedback on Another's Digital Project	56%
Revise Something Based on Others' Feedback	48%

Source: 2012 YOUmedia Survey

TABLE 11

Chapter 3: About Half of YOUmedia Teens Say They Live South or Southeast of the HWLC; Different than CPS High School Students Overall		
Primary Residence	YOUmedia (Percent of Teens)	CPS High School (Percent of Teens)
Downtown	2%	0%
North/Northwest	18%	36%
South/Southeast	54%	29%
Southwest	18%	29%
West	8%	6%

Source: 2012 YOUmedia Survey

TABLE 12

Chapter 3: YOUmedia Teen's Self-Reported Race/Ethnicity Differs from Typical CPS High School Students		
Race/Ethnicity	YOUmedia (Percent of Teens)	CPS High School (Percent of Teens)
Asian/Pacific Islander/Hawaiian	2%	4%
Bi-Racial/Multi-Racial	13%	1%
Black/African American	65%	46%
Latino/a	12%	41%
Native American/Alaskan Native/Other	1%	1%
White/Caucasian	7%	7%

Source: 2012 YOUmedia Survey

TABLE 13

Chapter 3: Typology of Teen Participation-Details					
	Percent of Teens				
	Socializers	**Readers/ Studiers**	**Floaters**	**Experimenters**	**Creators**
% of Sample	18%	28%	21%	11%	22%
Gender					
% Female	55%	45%	22%	26%	31%
Race/Ethnicity					
% African American	68%	71%	52%	65%	67%
% Latino/a	10%	16%	17%	9%	4%
% Other	22%	13%	31%	26%	29%
Age					
% 14-15	8%	16%	13%	30%	13%
% 16-17	80%	63%	63%	35%	51%
% 18-20	12%	21%	24%	35%	36%
Duration of Visits					
More than One Year	60%	57%	63%	39%	60%
One Year or Less	40%	43%	37%	61%	40%
Frequency/Length of Visits					
At Least Weekly/At Least One Hour	45%	46%	52%	61%	82%
At Least Weekly/Less than One Hour	25%	9%	15%	13%	9%
Twice per Month or Less/ Any Length	30%	45%	33%	26%	9%
Introduced to a New Interest	64%	61%	59%	78%	93%
Workshop Types					
Music Production	15%	14%	20%	52%	58%
Graphic Design	13%	13%	26%	26%	18%
Photography	13%	13%	22%	35%	9%
Film	8%	11%	11%	30%	22%
Poetry	18%	13%	24%	44%	29%
Reading or Writing	13%	11%	28%	22%	22%
Gaming	13%	16%	39%	48%	29%
Two or More Types	19%	18%	41%	56%	49%
Work with a Mentor on a Project					
At Least Weekly	10%	0%	4%	17%	43%
Monthly or Less	27%	25%	44%	35%	33%
Never	63%	75%	52%	48%	24%

Source: 2012 YOUmedia Survey

Endnotes

Introduction

1   Shelly, Cashman, Gunter, and Gunter (2007).

2   Ito, Gutiérrez, Livingstone, Penuel, Rhodes, Salen, Schor, Sefton-Green, and Watkins (2013) assert that digital and networked media have special relevance for Connected Learning.

3   Bushweller (2012).

4   CCSSO (2010).

5   NCES (2012).

6   The White House, Office of the Press Secretary, September 16, 2010.

7   Hannon (2007).

8   Austin, Ehrlich, Puckett, and Singleton (2011).

9   Austin et al. (2011).

10   Ito et al., Chapter 1 (2009).

11   Ito et al. (2013).

12   Developmental evaluation is not the same as process evaluation that focuses on the implementation of a clearly defined program. Questions addressed by process evaluation revolve around the qualities of a program's operation and whether the program is functioning as intended. Developmental evaluation is relevant to programs that are still being formed; questions vary and support ongoing change and adaptation. Patton (2011).

13   Ibid., Chapter 1.

14   Austin et al. (2011).

15   Austin et al. (2011).

16   Ito et al. (2013).

Chapter 1

17   See Hansen, Larson, and Dworkin (2003); and Deschenes, McDonald, and McLaughlin (2004). Both were cited in Deschenes, Arbreton, Little, Herrera, Grossman, and Weiss (2010).

18   See Fredericks and Eccles (2006), cited in Deschenes et al. (2010).

19   Ito et al. (2013).

20   Ito et al. (2009).

21   Austin et al. (2011).

22   http://www.chipublib.org/aboutcpl/index.php.

23   http://www.digitalyouthnetwork.org/1-about/pages/1-overview.

24   Austin et al. (2011).

25   Partnerships developed more or less organically based on the connections made by the MacArthur Foundation and the YOUmedia staff. The Foundation established its own partnership with Lady Gaga's Born This Way Foundation, and several projects followed from this. YOUmedia's participation in the What's Going On... Now project resulted from a chance meeting between a staff member from the DYN and arts administrators from the Kennedy Center at the annual Digital Media and Learning Conference. The connection of another YOUmedia staff member led to a partnership with Vocalo.org 89.5 FM, a Chicago public radio station geared toward younger audiences. Through this partnership, teens who participated in the podcasting and online literary magazine workshops at YOUmedia visited the Vocalo studios, where they learned about professional opportunities for broadcast and online print journalism. Some YOUmedia teen podcasts and videos were featured on Vocalo's website.

26   Austin et al. (2011).

Chapter 2

27   Fashiola (2003).

28   See companion report on technology use in CPS. Ehrlich, Sporte, and Sebring (2013).

29   Deschenes (2010).

30   Lee (2012).

31   Collection of museums, schools, libraries, and other non-profit groups serving youth. They are dedicated to providing teens opportunities to pursue their interests online and in physical spaces. Activities range from science projects to youth media production to the arts. YOUmedia is a member of the Hive Learning Network. For more information, visit http://www.hivelearning-network.org/about/mission.

32   Akili Lee, CEO and President of Remix Learning, provided background on the evolution of the YOUmedia social network (2013).

33   Lee (2013).

Chapter 4

34 Austin et al. (2011).

35 Strobel, Kirshner, O'Donoghue, and McLaughlin (2008).

36 Herr-Stephenson, Rhoten, Perkel, and Sims (2011).

37 Austin et al. (2011).

Chapter 5

38 Ehrlich, Sporte, and Sebring (2013).

39 Fashiola (2003).

40 Ito et al. (2013).

41 Ito, Gutiérrez, Livingston, Penuel, Rhodes, Salen, Schor, Sefton-Green, and Watkins (2013).

42 This is borrowed from Ito et al. (2013), p. 63.

43 Ito et al. (2013).

44 Deschenes, Arbreton, Little, Herrera, Grossman, and Weiss (2010).

45 Duncan and Murnane (2011).

46 Ito et al. (2013), pp. 78-81.

47 Ehrlich et al. (2013).

48 Ehrlich et al. (2013).

ABOUT THE AUTHORS

PENNY BENDER SEBRING is a Senior Research Associate at the University of Chicago and Founding Co-Director of UChicago CCSR. She is currently leading research on YOUmedia Chicago and she is co-author of *Organizing Schools for Improvement: Lessons from Chicago* (University of Chicago Press, 2010). She graduated with a BA in sociology from Grinnell College, where she is a life member of the Board of Trustees. She received a PhD in education and policy studies from Northwestern University. Sebring serves on the Board of Directors for the Chicago Public Education Fund and she is Chair of the Policy Advisory Board of the School of Education and Social Policy at Northwestern University.

ERIC BROWN is a first-year PhD student in the School of Education and Social Policy at Northwestern University. Eric is interested in researching how peers, family, school, and community affect the development of noncognitive behaviors for urban adolescent youth. He worked at UChicago CCSR for four years prior to beginning his studies at Northwestern. His other research projects at UChicago CCSR include the Focus on Freshman project, the evaluation of the Excellence in Teaching Pilot study, and working with a network of schools in Chicago's Woodlawn community. Eric is especially proud of his involvement on the YOUmedia study, as the project uniquely drew upon his research background and experiences as a social worker with adolescent youth.

KATE JULIAN is a Senior Research Associate at Evanston Township High School in Evanston, Illinois. She has led both internal and external program evaluations of high school reform initiatives and after-school programs. Previously, she was a middle grades teacher. She received a PhD in educational psychology from the University of Illinois at Chicago.

STACY B. EHRLICH is a Senior Research Analyst at UChicago CCSR. Along with studying how Chicago teens interact with digital media and technology, she is conducting research on the effects of early chronic absenteeism in CPS. Prior work, at Education Development Center, Inc. (EDC),

included conducting research responding to states' educational policy concerns and a study on a preschool science professional development program. Ehrlich earned her BS in human development and family studies from the University of Wisconsin-Madison and an MA and PhD in developmental psychology from the University of Chicago.

SUSAN E. SPORTE is Director for Research Operations at UChicago CCSR. Her current research focuses on teacher preparation and measuring effective teaching. She serves as the main point of contact with Chicago Public Schools regarding data sharing and research priorities; she also oversees UChicago CCSR's data archive. Prior to joining UChicago CCSR, she worked as a community college math instructor, field evaluator for a not-for-profit agency, and college administrator. Sporte received a BS in mathematics from Michigan State University, an MA in mathematics from the University of Illinois–Springfield, and an EdM and EdD in administration, planning, and social policy from the Harvard Graduate School of Education.

ERIN BRADLEY was a Research Assistant at UChicago CCSR. She currently works as the Chicago Project Coordinator for the Connecting Youth: Digital Learning Research Project at New York University, which studies youth, educators, and organizations involved in digital media and education. She earned her BA from Illinois Wesleyan University and her MA in social service administration from the University of Chicago.

LISA MEYER was a research assistant at UChicago CCSR. She currently works at Inspiration Corporation, a nonprofit social service agency for individuals who are homeless or at risk of homelessness. She develops relationships with businesses and coordinates a collaborative of 40-plus nonprofits across the Chicago area that works to connect disadvantaged job seekers to employment. She received a BA in sociology and Spanish from Furman University and an MA in social service administration from the University of Chicago.

UCHICAGOCCSR

CONSORTIUM ON CHICAGO SCHOOL RESEARCH